D1825169

SHETLAND

AN ILLUSTRATED ARCHITECTURAL —— GUIDE ——

SHETLAND marks another milestone in the award-winning RIAS/Landmark Trust series of Illustrated Architectural Guides to Scotland. It offers the opportunity of a fuller appreciation of these historical islands at the most northerly edge of the British Isles. At the crossroads of the North Atlantic, invaders, settlers and traders have each left their mark on the landscape and spectacular scenery of the Shetlands. Bronze Age settlements, mysterious brochs built by the Picts, wooden Viking houses, 17th century Baltic trading bases, Cromwellian fortifications up to the recent growth associated with the oil industry, record Shetland's history.

After centuries of absorbing and adapting to incoming cultural influences, the Shetland Isles have evolved a unique identity captured in this volume.

CHARLES MACDONELL
PAST PRESIDENT
Inverness Architectural Association

© Author: *Michael Finnie*
Series editor: *Charles McKean*
Series consultant: *David Walker*
Cover design: *Dorothy Steedman*
Editorial consultant: *Duncan McAra*

Mainstream Publications (Scotland) Ltd.
Royal Incorporation of Architects in Scotland
ISBN 185158 390 4
First Published 1990

Cover illustrations:
Michael Finnie

Typesetting and page make-up: Trinity Typesetting, Edinburgh
Printed by Pillans & Wilson Ltd., Edinburgh

A

INTRODUCTION

The 100 or so islands which make up Shetland lie to the north of mainland Scotland, beyond Orkney. Aberdeen, the main transport terminus on the Scottish mainland, lies 200 miles south. Bergen in Norway is about 220 miles to the east. Rocky, uncompromising islands — the land is hilly but never reaches any great height. Ronas Hill, the highest, is 1486 ft.

One-third of the islands' population is concentrated in the capital, and only town, Lerwick. The only other settlements with any considerable population are Scalloway, the ancient capital, and Brae which expanded rapidly in the 1970s to acommodate an oil-related influx. Elsewhere the land follows a crofting pattern of individual cottages scattered over the inbye land or in loose townships.

These distant islands, far to the north, though part of Scotland, remain distinct from it and unfamiliar to most UK citizens. This far-flung outpost, now remote from the centres of power, is at the crossroads of shipping routes in the North Sea and North Atlantic.

In Norse times, Shetland was a stepping stone between Norway and the other centres of the Nordic world — Iceland, Orkney, Hebrides, Dublin and Man. So familiar was Shetland to the Norse that these islands were considered an extension of the Norwegian homeland. While Orkney looked south towards Scotland, Shetland looked east. The *Orkneyinga Saga*, written by an Icelandic historian, relates the events of the Orkney Earls up to the 13th century. Shetland plays only a minor part in the story, lacking the colour and life of the Orkney court. We get the impression of a stable farming community. With such a down-to-earth working population,. often under the influence of outsiders, the islands' buildings have never reached the grandeur which power and wealth might have brought.

Always the natural stone predominates in workaday buildings dependent on the limited materials available and cowing to the harsh environment. From the earliest settlers, during whose time the islands' tree cover disappeared, timber has been restricted to driftwood and costly imports. The Norse brought wood over from Norway and this tradition continued until the 19th century when prefabricated boat kits were brought over the North Sea. This restriction to the limited locally available resources resulted in buildings notably in

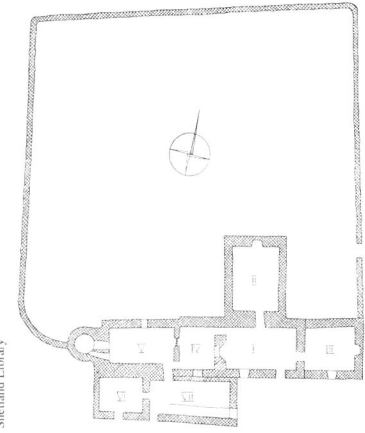

Shetland Library

Farm at Skelberry, South Mainland from Roussel 'Norse Building Customs in the Scottish Isles' 1934. Left *Mousa Broch (Finnie)*

Croft houses are scattered over the fertile areas of the islands. The Norse brought rectilinear buildings which contrast with the round houses of the Iron Age. Medieval rectangular longhouses with side rooms and smaller outhouses were built from stone and turf, although better buildings used timber from Norway for internal framing and lining. By the early 19th century, the longhouse was being replaced by cottages with low stone walls, and turf and straw-covered roofs. These cottages housed an increasing population on subdivided parcels of land provided by landlords, whose prime concern was labour to man their fishing boats and curing beaches. The 19th-century arrangement consisted, typically, of house, barn and byre in two oblong buildings, parallel and attached to each other with the entrance through the byre. Fires were in the beaten earth floor, smoke escaping through holes in the roof. From the mid-1800s, wall heads were often heightened to accommodate attic rooms (with rooflights rather than dormers), gable chimneys added, windows replaced holes in the roof and the interiors were given timber floors and lined walls. Wood and tarred felt began to replace thatch, slate being reserved for the wealthy and the church. Shetland was left with a range of buildings which were not to undergo major changes until new-found prosperity in the 1970s.

As an outlandish destination
Shetland attracted early travellers.
Regular sailings to the islands did
not exist until the 19th century;
before then only the adventurous
and persistent managed the trip
which may have involved the
crossing from Orkney in an open
boat. To these adventurers,
Shetland's seabound scenery was
spectacular and her people and
customs curious. The Cradle of Noss,
considered almost as one of the
wonders of the Northern World, was
the goal of many travellers. Tourism
increased after Sir Walter Scott, who
visited in 1814, illuminated his
novel *The Pirate*, with his
observations of the scenery, customs
and people.

Privateers, from as far as France
and America, harassed the men of
Shetland during the 18th century.
From 1755 the Royal Navy
considered the islands a prime area
for the press gang: '. . . *the great
advantage ... is that every
Shetlander, man and boy,
understands how to handle an oar
and manage a ship.*' During the
Napoleonic Wars up to 2000
Shetlanders served in the Royal
Navy, many impressed.

harmony with the landscape: low ground-
hugging crofthouses set under a wide sky and
the well-defined homogeneity of Lerwick's
waterfront.

But Shetland's isolation — which has resulted
in a distinctive flora and diminutive fauna — did
not preclude southern influences from being felt.
Scalloway and Muness (Unst) have fine
examples of Scots tower houses. With limited
resources the lairds emulated southern fashions.
Lunna (East Mainland) retains a grand axis and
the laird of Belmont (Unst) embarked on a grand
tour, albeit to Lothian, before building his house
(*c.*1777). Embellishment was (as it generally
remains) an unwarranted luxury.

Shetland's fortunes have long depended on the
sea — whereas the Orcadian is said to be a
crofter with a boat, his Shetland equivalent is a
fisherman with a croft, for ever since it became
possible to cure fish for preservation, fishing has
been a mainstay of these islands. Prosperity has
come in waves and as one source of income
receded another arrived. The herring fishery
boomed in the late 19th century replacing the
earlier cod. Oil in the 1970s caused an
unprecedented growth, but as the present
fishing industry faces declining stocks and
restricted quotas, Shetland's voes are filling with
the cages of farmed salmon.

Ness Yoals at Spiggie

Shetland Museum

4

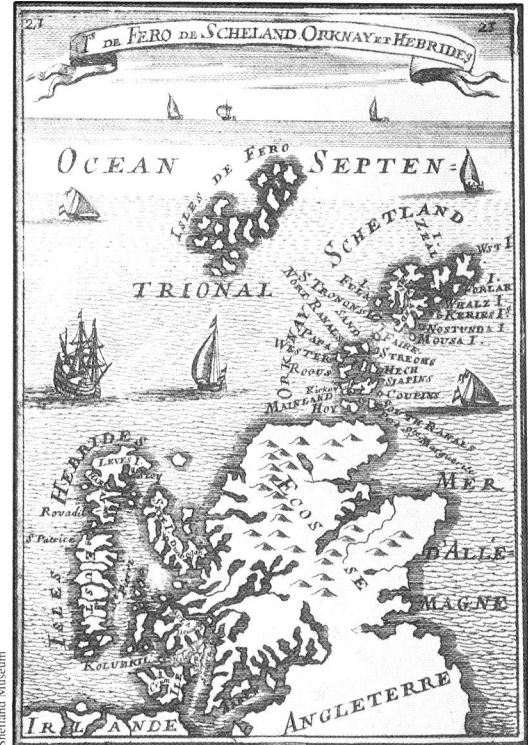

Shetland Museum

Shetland's position in relation to Scotland, Orkney and Faroe by Alain Manesson Mallet, 1683.

Norse heritage remains in the names of the majority of geographical features and places. Church parishes follow the Norse divisions of the lands. Delting, Nesting, Aithsting and Sandsting etc. commemorate the ting, or law court, of each district with the supreme court, the lawting, at Tingwall. Prominent are the many voes, the Norse word for these sea inlets penetrating deep into the land. Whilst much Nordic influence remains, some is the result of a later, Victorian, fervour for the past. From the latter part of the last century come the Norse street names of Lerwick's New Town and the present form of the winter fire festival of *Up Helly Aa*.

'...*If there were only trees and sun, no abode would be so sweet; but if they had trees and sun all the world would wish to go there and the peace would be no more*'
Jean-Baptiste Biot, 1817

'*There is a beauty that tears at you, and yet it is so often marred by buildings or construction work of breathtaking ugliness.*
Liv Kjorsvik Schei, 1988

This guide is intended as an introduction to the character and history of Shetland through the medium of its architectural heritage. The aim is to illustrate the building types constructed by people at each stage of the islands' settlement. Thus we gain an insight into the aspirations of the builders, their power and wealth and the society of the period. The guide does not list all deserving buildings, but includes prime examples of each particular type. Every effort has been made to ensure accuracy. Many people have assisted in this publication (see p.94) but the responsibility for inaccuracies remains with the author who would welcome corrections.

Sequence
This guide covers the archipelago of Shetland — a land area of 1426 sq km (550 sq miles) with a vastly disproportionate coastline. Although at no point is the land more than 3 miles from sea, distances are surprisingly large, distorted by the popular image of the islands squeezed — often at a reduced scale — into a box, adrift in varied locations off the British Coast.

Shetland, published in 1711

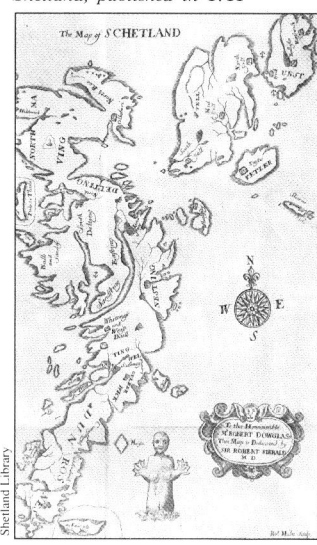

Shetland Library

'Up Helly Aa' galley on display prior to its spectacular demise

We begin in **Lerwick**, capital and metropolis. Here one may arrive by sea, as one should in these seafaring islands. First, the older town, founded on fishing, followed by the new town, funded by fishing, with newer development and the very ancient at Clickimin Broch on the periphery. We then move out to the **Central Mainland**, a rather loosely defined area, then **Scalloway**, the former capital. The remainder of Mainland is divided into rather convenient lumps: **South Mainland's** long leg stretching to Sumburgh, the mass of voes and lochs of the **West Mainland**, the **East Mainland** coast and the **North Mainland**. Thereafter the islands. The larger North Isles of **Yell**, **Unst** and **Fetlar**. Then **Whalsay** and **Out Skerries** off the east coast and **Bressay**, the vital bulwark to Lerwick harbour. And off the west coast **Papa Stour**, **Trondra** and **Burra**. Finally, the two outlying fragments **Fair Isle** and **Foula**.

Text Arrangement

Entries for principal buildings follow the sequence of name (or number), address, date and architect (if known). Lesser buildings are contained within paragraphs. Demolished buildings are included if appropriate. Text in the small column is illustrative of less architectural aspects of the story of Shetland.

Sponsors

This Guide would have been impossible had it not been for the kind support of sponsors, pre-eminent amongst them Shetland Arts Trust, Shetland Civic Trust, Shetland Amenity Trust, the Landmark Trust and the Highlands & Islands Development Board. Fundamentally, it is that financial assistance which enabled volumes such as this to be published at a low sale price.

Access to properties

Many of the buildings described in this guide are open to the public, or are visible from a public road or footpath. Some are private, and readers are requested to respect the occupiers' privacy.

Map References

Maps of Shetland, Lerwick's outer and inner areas and Scalloway are included. The numbers relate to references in the text itself. Owing to the area covered, the map of Shetland can give no more than general locations.

Lying in the path of Viking expansion westwards, Shetland had established Norse settlements before the 9th century. Originally part of the Norse Earldom of Orkney, Shetland reverted to direct administration from Norway following Earl Harald's involvement in a failed attempt to depose the Norwegian King Sverre in 1194. The 13th century saw Norway's hold over her southern possessions weaken; she gave up Man and the Hebrides but retained the Northern Isles. In the fourteenth century Norway herself became subject to Danish rule.

A marriage treaty was arranged in 1468 between James III of Scotland and Margaret, Princess of Denmark. The dowry was 60,000 florins of which 10,000 were to be paid within the year and the crown lands of Orkney pledged for the remainder. Denmark's finances were strained after war against Sweden and only 2000 florins were paid in time. Shetland was pawned for the remaining 8000, in 1469, under the condition that she should revert back on payment of the debt and that under Scots rule she should enjoy her own customs and laws. The following year Earl William St Clair of Orkney gave up his rights to the Earldom in favour of King James III and in 1471 the isles were annexed to Scotland.

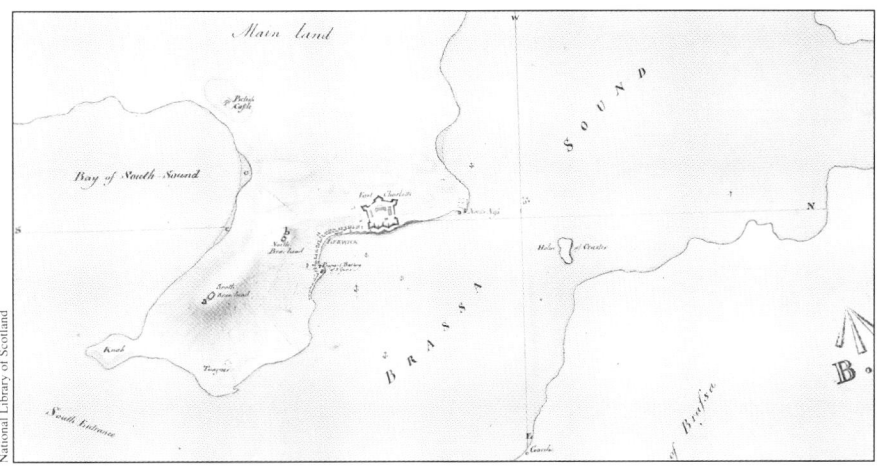

National Library of Scotland

LERWICK

Shetland's capital is not ancient, barely 350 years old. In the early 17th century, it was still *leir-vik* — Norse for mud bay. North-east facing (thus exposed to chill winds) with a poor hinterland, Lerwick was not founded for its prime location within the isles nor for any wealth of agriculture but for convenience. The sandy bay on Bressay Sound was to prove ideal for serving the Dutch fishing fleet offshore. A collection of huts sprang up and became notorious for immorality and drunkenness at the annual Dutch fair, '... *the great abomination and wickedness committed yearly by the Hollanders and country people, godless and profane persons repairing to them at the houses of Lerwick ...*' The authorities at Scalloway, the ancient capital, ordered these shanties to be '*utterlie dimolished and downe cassin to the ground*'. Doubtless they were soon resurrected.

The potential of Bressay Sound, and its importance to the Dutch state, was soon realised. Cromwell's troops garrisoned Scalloway Castle, and began the erection of Fort Charlotte against a possible invasion by the Dutch. Lerwick grew along the shoreline below, consolidated by an influx of southern merchants in the latter half of the 17th century. But the destruction of the Dutch fleet by the French in 1703 was to deprive the town of much of its income, and rural lairds deprived the growing town of trade when they set up the 'truck' system whereby tenants were forced to trade exclusively from them. Only once the Dutch

Plan of Bressay Sound with Fort Charlotte drawn by Lt-Col Frazer, 1783

'It is a most beautiful place, screened on all sides from the wind by hills of gentle elevation. The town, a fishing village built irregularly upon a hill ascending from the shore, has a picturesque appearance.'
Walter Scott, 1814

While there are tales of Lerwick
Recalled and handed down,
Lives on the Northern Venice,
The little, old, grey town.
from **Northern Venice** by 'Vagaland' (T A Robertson)

'. . . *the town* is so remarkably striking, that woe betide the Hyperborean architects who would reduce the irregular lines of its street, on which its picturesque appearance depends, to the dull uniformity of right lines and squares.'
Samuel Hibbert, 1822

'**The houses** stand with tall gable ends towards the sea, which many of them overhang in such a way that the very cooks' maids could catch podlies from their kitchen windows.'
James Wilson, 1841

'**The Citadel** has never been finished, but in case of publick disturbance has the command of the whole Sound, and might soon be put in such repair as render it highly useful for the protection of the fishing trade particularly.'
Revd G Low, 1774

Governor of Faroe

In 1839 Faroe was a poor colony of Denmark. Christian Ployen, the Danish Governor of Faroe, arrived in Lerwick, to study the fisheries and agriculture, on 5 June, as part of a fact-finding tour of Shetland, Orkney and Scotland: '. . . *I certainly expected to find Shetland far before Faroe, but I did not imagine that the inhabitants of the first-named islands would be in possession of all the comforts and luxuries ... Everything made me feel that I had come to the land of opulence.*'

Faroe had only infrequent communications with Denmark and Ployen found that '*Shetland has the great privilege, that every Sunday morning a large steam vessel (the Sovereign) comes from Edinburgh to Lerwick ...*'

Bressay Sound

' ... *a capacious bay, in which vessels, well found, may ride at all season in perfect safety; and what renders this harbour particularly commodious, is, its having two entries, one from the south and another from the north.*'
Revd Thomas Barclay, 1841

Lerwick drawn in 1766 by William Aberdeen. Three 'trances' can be seen bridging Commercial Street which has assumed its present form

King Herring

The herring industry boomed from 1875 with curing stations throughout the islands and two major centres at Baltasound and Lerwick, the latter finally dominating. Following the seasonal migration of the herring, Scots, English, Irish, Dutch and Scandinavian boats converged. At the peak of activity, tales tell of being able to walk across the decks from Lerwick to Bressay. Following the fleet, came thousands of gutters and packers to work at the many stations, splitting and packing the fish with salt into barrels. Accommodation was in the many gutter huts, little more than wooden sheds, of which few remain.

resumed fishing did the town pick up. It grew slowly though the 18th century, gaining in status by breaking away from Tingwall to become a separate parish with its own church and tolbooth. Fort Charlotte was reconstructed and garrisoned in 1781, and during the Napoleonic Wars, from 1799 to 1815, rapid growth brought the population from about 900 to over 2000. Building crowded behind the street and up steep lanes (called closses), poor and wealthy living cheek by jowl. A pattern of simple stone houses providing maximum accommodation, gables to the street in feus, became firmly established. The narrowness of the street, lanes and enclosed spaces also gave shelter from the chill Arctic winds sweeping in from the north.

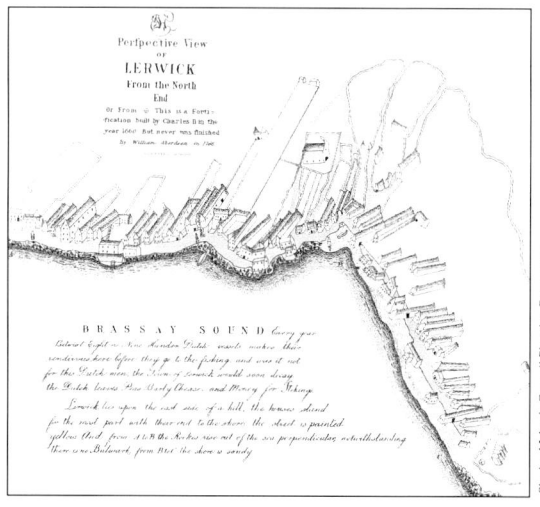

Shetland Islands Council Planning Department

The town expanded in the early 1800s when local merchants (such as Hay and Ogilvy) founded and developed herring curing yards, boatyards, docks and warehouses based upon an increasing trade with the south. Poorer fishing around 1840 slowed the rate of development, but income was to come from the continuing Dutch trade and from Greenland whalers *en route* to spend the summer in Arctic waters. Whalers came to Lerwick from Peterhead, Aberdeen, Dundee, Hull and other ports, to take on stores and hire Shetland men as crew. A further boom in Lerwick's fortunes came in 1875 with King Herring. At herring's peak in 1905, Lerwick was Britain's busiest herring port, and curing stations extended north from the North Ness.

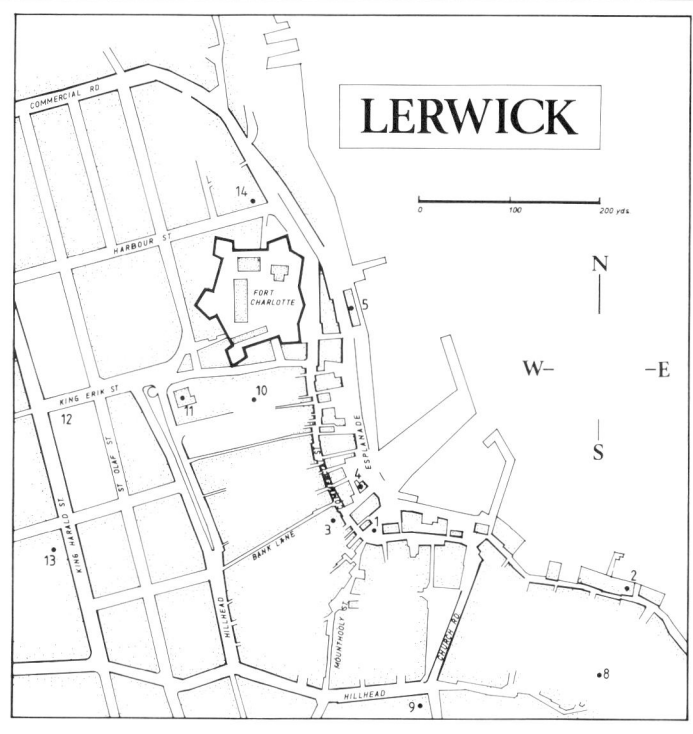

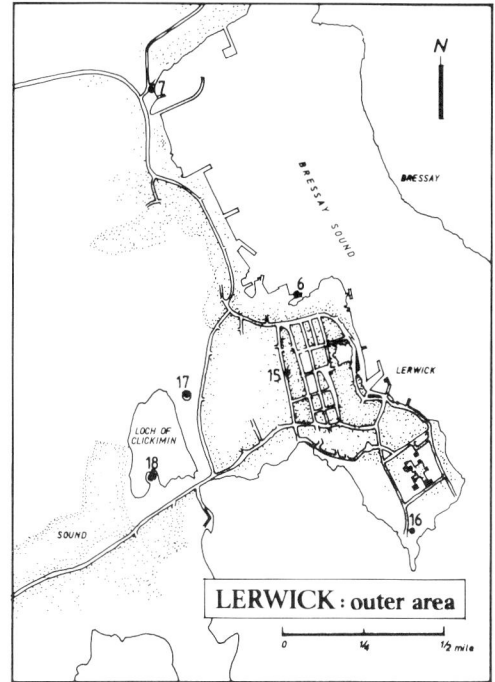

National Library of Scotland

RCAHMS

Shetland Museum

Finnie

Top *Lerwick, drawn in 1848, after J. C. Schetky.* Above *Lerwick, drawn from below Fort Charlotte by John Irvine c.1840.* Middle left *Lerwick by Skene of Rubislaw, early 19th century.* Left *Lerwick's waterfront drawn by John Irvine c.1840*

Herring had brought money enough to finance Lerwick's New Town, whose open grid-iron layout was as much a reaction against the constricted lanes and all that was backward, as it was a symbol of civic wealth.

From the 1920s Lerwick's poor were at last given the opportunity to quit the cramped lanes and move into new houses, first at Breiwick and later in a massive belt from Burgh Road to Clickimin. This exodus left the centre to decay, and only in the last 20 years has the inner area risen in status and attraction.

North Sea Oil was to be Lerwick's next saviour, development bursting the town's bounds north and south — industry and oilfield servicing northwards, and housing sprawl on the southern approach. The construction period was to overtake any thoughts which might have been given to the advice from the *Architectural Review* in 1969 that the town 'Halt expansion west and instead build up the waterside on the north end of the town.' Clickimin Broch's setting was compromised. Earlier periods had resulted in defined and identifiable areas: the Old and New Towns and even the council housing. The latter part of the 20th century has left little more than a ragged frill around the town.

Strategically important in the North Atlantic, Bressay Sound has played host to voyagers from earliest times. King Harald Hardrada of Norway stopped in Shetland on his way to defeat at Stamford Bridge in 1066, and later King Hakon sheltered before his defeat at the battle of Largs. In 1904, the German fleet was given the freedom of the port — a decision later regretted, when during the First World War Allied convoys assembled here. Ever cosmopolitan, Lerwick's harbour continues to host shipping from throughout Northern Europe and beyond.

Commercial Street

As its name suggests, Commercial Street is the place of banks, hotels, post office, business premises — the hub of the town. It once hugged the shoreline with lodberries built out into the sea, but reclamation has pushed the shoreline beyond reach, and it retains intimacy with the sea only at the South End. It is the irregularity, the simple forms, the stunning textures and the shelter afforded or exposure threatened which make being on the street an experience.

However, Lerwick is a seaport, and colour and activity from the harbour is glimpsed between buildings, and life trickles in through lanes.

Up Helly Aa
Yuletide was celebrated, until 1874, by burning tar barrels being pulled through the streets. As behaviour tended towards the riotous, the tar barrels were banned. The *Up Helly Aa* celebration as such appeared in 1881 with a torchlight procession. At the suggestion of J Haldane Burgess, a Shetland scholar of Norse mythology, the first longship appeared eight years later. Always held on the last Tuesday in January and with never a postponement for weather. In the dark northern night, hundreds of torchbearers march through the streets of the New Town to assemble for the climax when the burning of the galley emulates the Norse Jarl's final journey to Valhalla.

'Lerwick, a poor-looking place — the streets flagged instead of being causewayed, for there are no wheel-carriages.'
Walter Scott, 1814

Commercial Street's stone flags had been replaced sadly by concrete imitations — but the lanes retain theirs; quarried in Bressay until that source dried up, and from 1910, Mousa.

Finnie

Finnie

Finnie

Top *Market Cross*. Middle
Commercial Street. Above *67
Commercial Street*

1 **Market Cross**
Little more than a widening of Commercial
Street opened to the harbour. An irregular
space, buzzing with activity, it replaced
Scalloway in the late 1830s as the place for
proclamations. The Cross itself, a dumpy
classical column of no great antiquity, comes
into its own in darkest January as the display
place for the *Up Helly Aa* proclamation.

Gabled frontages from the 18th and 19th
centuries line the landward side of the street.
No 99, *c.*1820, has the remains of a moulded
doorway stranded high up on the north side, the
forestair gone. The street widens in response to
the stiff formality of the **Royal Bank of
Scotland**, 1871, David Rhind. Constructed
originally as the Commercial Bank, it comprises
three floors of modest Banker's Italianate.

No 67 Commercial Street, 19th century
This has an elegant bowed gable ending the
street before Church Road slices a swathe
through. Formerly the street broadened into a
roughly triangular space, the 'half-napkin',
fronting the **Tolbooth**, 1767-70. The present
tolbooth replaced a 17th-century predecessor.
McGibbon and Ross, in 1892, thought the
Tolbooth rather old fashioned: '*the style of the
seventeenth century took a considerable time to
reach the Shetlands.*' A plain two-storey block
distinguished by corner quoins and scrolled
skewputts. The removal, in 1927, of the clock
tower was lamentable.

Finnie

Shetland Museum

Top *Lerwick Tolbooth, drawn by McGibbon & Ross in 1892.* Bottom *The street side of the Post Office.* Above *Commercial Street looking north towards the tolbooth with its clock tower c.1895*

Finnie

Post Office, 1910, W T Oldrieve of the Board of Works, assisted by A R Myres
Self-assured, colourful Scots Renaissance, creamy render contrasted with red Eday (Orkney) sandstone. Outstanding civic design with crowsteps, a balustraded tower and boat-gabled dormers.

Queen's Hotel, 1860s
Two- and three-storey buildings incorporating Yate's and Hay's lodberries.

The **Post Office** was built over Sinclair's Beach. In 1887 Andrew Smith won in a dispute with Lerwick Harbour Trust over ownership of the beach. Udal (Norse) Law, whereby the landowner owns the foreshore triumphed over Scots Law where the foreshore is Crown property.

Stout's Pier was built by the father of Sir Robert Stout. Emigrating to New Zealand, Robert studied law and was elected a member of the New Zealand Parliament, before becoming Prime Minister in 1884.

RCAHMS

Top *The Lodberry* Above *Quendale House*

Lodberries are one of the main features of Lerwick's waterfront. The word originally meant a flat rock that could be used as a natural landing place, and hence, when constructed, applied to a small private pier which could be used for unloading goods from a boat to the courtyard of a merchant's house. The word has now become the name by which these merchants' stores are known, particularly where the waterfront reclamation has resulted in the loss of the piers and courtyards.

Seafield House, No 49, 18th century
The town house of Ogilvy of Seafield in Yell. One of a splendid parade of narrow-gabled fronts.

Lochend House, No 41, *c.*1760
Another town house — for the merchant family of Nicolson. The greater part is back from the street, one wing with a crowstepped gable.
The sandy **Bain's Beach** opposite has escaped development. Flats, on a partly piloti'd ground floor, at the foot of **Water Lane** form part of the Greenfield development, 1965, Richard Moira.

The Lodberry, 18th century
Highly picturesque, house, stores and a ventilated fish-drying house, with battered walls which drop from the street to sea level, water enclosing it on three sides.

Quendale House, 1865
Rises, aloof, above the humbler buildings around with a formal rhythm of multiple windows. This was the town residence of a laird, Andrew Grierson of Quendale.
After **Craigie Stane**, another beach, Commercial Street squeezes between properties. Those seaward, with lodberries and tiny courts, were prime properties for trading, and, at one time, for illicit importing. Periodic collapses of the street have revealed tunnels with smuggling connections.

Lerwick Boating Club, tucked between 12 & 14 Commercial Street, 1983, Richard Moira. Only a massive concrete corbel indicates that this is a new-built lodberry. Glazed frontage to the sea. **Hayfield Court**, *c.*1800, lies gable-end to the street with a lush walled garden.

14

Finnie

Dennis Coutts

Shetland Museum

Left *10 Commercial Street.*. Top *Leog housing before re-roofing.* Above *Widows' Homes, with their flèche intact*

² **10 Commercial Street**, *c.*1730 and renovated 1988 by Richard Gibson
One of the town's earliest houses. When built by Patrick Torry it was the only house on the seaward side of the street. A two-and-a-half-storey merchant's house with thick rendered walls. Projecting stone slabs shed water from above openings and protect the crowsteps.

Opposite are more piloti'd flats, 1966, by Richard Moira.

2-8 Commercial Street, *c.*1817
A rubble tenement with Stout's and Copeland's lodberries and piers on the sea side.

Old Manse, 9 Commercial Street, *c.*1685
Lerwick's oldest house, its antiquity somewhat obscured by a Victorian porch.

Leog Housing, 1961, Richard Moira
A mixed infill scheme of single- and two-storey houses in render and rubble. The original felted butterfly roofs have been replaced by conventional pitched and tiled. The garage of **The Knowe** makes conspicuous use of an upturned boat for its roof.

Anderson Homes, former Widows' Homes, Twageos Road, 1865
A benevolent gift from Arthur Anderson in memory of his wife, intended originally for the widows of seamen. Fitting Gothic almshouse.

Trances
In the restricted space of 18th-century Lerwick, gabled properties bridged Commercial Street to give merchants access to the sea and increased accommodation. The passages under were called trances. Three are shown in William Aberdeen's view of Lerwick in 1766.

Richard Moira, 1901-88
In 1949, the Edinburgh architect Richard Moira was commissioned to prepare a Burgh Plan for Lerwick, with a view to regenerating the inner areas of the town rather than build on new greenfield sites. Moira was commissioned subsequently to design infill schemes for locations identified in the plan. A succession of award-winning schemes followed at **Heddel's Park** (1956), **Greenfield** (1965) and **Leog** (1961).

RCAHMS

Shetland Museum

Finnie

Right *Commercial Street c.1895.* Top *Bank of Scotland photographed in 1959.* Above *Grand Hotel's tower rising over Commercial Street*

3 Bank of Scotland, 117 Commercial Street
1906, J J Burnet
An outburst of gorgeous baroque in warm ashlar. The front is richly modelled, and attached Ionic columns and pilasters support a deep cornice and barrel-roofed pediment. Expanses of render at the sides set off elegant sweeping railings and hint at more to come on the rear elevation. Here is Queen Anne revival style with beaten metalwork, a bow window and steep gables.

Grand Hotel, 145-151 Commercial Street
1887, William Hamilton Beattie
The architect of Edinburgh's North British hotel brought the Scots Baronial style (considered appropriate in those days for a transport terminus) with all the familiar elements in its tall frontage. (Lerwick's John M Aitken was the contractor). A rope-bound doorway fails to fit in, sliced off by the square tower the base of which is the earlier 'Stoot's Hoose'.

90 Commercial Street (J G Rae & Manson), *c.*1900, John M Aitken
Low and heavily burdened by castellated detail. Note the portcullis doorway and the barley-sugar rain-water pipes. Townscape is at its best where the street sidesteps past the **Bradford &**

In **'Stoot's Hoose**' during the mid 1800s a Mr Leask ran a shipping agent's business; his office was frequently packed with men waiting to sign on for the Greenland whaling.

Commercial Street drawn by Laura Stewart Sandison

Bingley Building Society, 159 Commercial Street. **No 98** has a Venetian window taking up most of the upper floor.

Clydesdale Bank, 106 Commercial Street, 1892, John M Aitken
A plain building adorned by crowstepped gables and pepperpot turrets. Good gables again at **Nos 173 and 175 Commercial Street** which then continues on reclaimed land below the walls of **Fort Charlotte** (originally a cliff face falling to the sea).

Fishermen's Mission, 1962, Leonard F Ivall
Sits in hideous opposition to the fort wall. Period cladding panels and spindly ironwork may once again come to be appreciated.

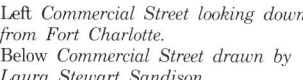

Left *Commercial Street looking down from Fort Charlotte.*
Below *Commercial Street drawn by Laura Stewart Sandison*

RCAHMS

Finnie

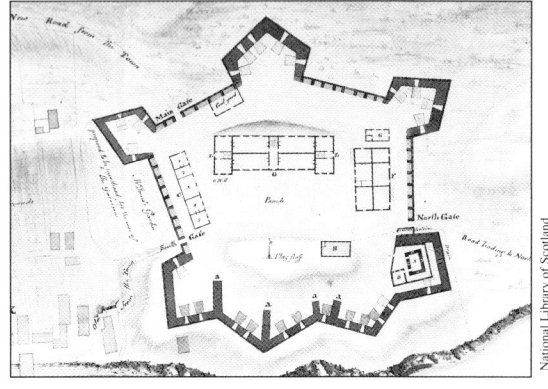

National Library of Scotland

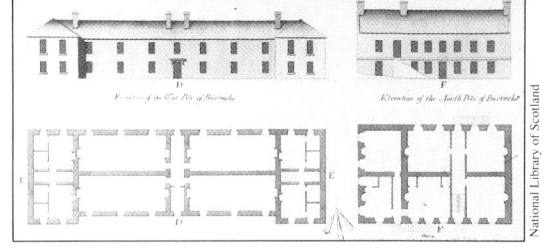

National Library of Scotland

Top *Fort Charlotte, hemmed in, the pentagon only seen from above.* Centre *Fort Charlotte drawn in 1783 by Lt-Col Frazer.* Right *Barracks, Fort Charlotte drawn by Lt-Col Frazer in 1786.* Above *The Southern Gate into Fort Charlotte*

Fort Charlotte

'Here is a fort at Lerwick on the West-side of Bressa built at the Kings Matie's expense anno 1660, the Houses theirin were burnt by the Hollander anno 1673.'

An irregular pentagonal fort built in 1665-7 by John Mylne, Master Mason to King Charles II, it was intended to protect shipping during the war with the Dutch. The east wall, where most firepower was needed, is angled and housed nine gun ports. Five bastions defend the landward sides providing crossfire. But all this failed to prevent the Dutch from burning the fort and much of the town on 13 August 1673. The fort lay in ruins until 1782, when Lt-Col Frazer, Chief Engineer in Scotland, created the parade of buildings within. It was then named after Queen Charlotte, wife of King George III.

Three gates led into the 18th-century fort. The main gate, to the west, led by way of Shetland's first road to the Knab. Three main ranges of buildings around the parade ground provide barracks, officers' accommodation, store and kitchen. The central barrack block is a restrained classical frontage, 11 bays long. The two bays at either end are heightened and slightly advanced. Buttresses inside the fort wall supported a wooden platform for musketry, *'As neither Earth nor Sod could be got to make Parapets in the Curtains ...'* The fort is jostled by later Lerwick and its exposed clifftop setting compromised by reclamation and road building below. Indeed it is easily forgotten that the cliff formerly fell to the sea, such is the bustle below. Aloof, the windswept parade ground still commands the town and Bressay Sound. Secret grassy bastions lie hidden in the farthest corners. Lerwick's greatest potential asset remains under-used and under-appreciated.

Great Fisherie

'In all publick Dutch writs the Herring fishing is called the Great Fisherie, whilst all others are called only the Small Fisheries.'

From the 1500s, when vast shoals of herring were found in Shetland waters, the Dutch fleet assembled in Bressay Sound prior to the fishing season beginning on Johnsmas (24 June). All had been made possible by the 15th-century discovery of a method of curing herring in barrels with salt. The wealth gained funded the rise of the Netherlands and the creation of their East and West Indian Empires — *'The principal Mine and chief Support of these Countries'.*

Central to the economy of the Dutch, Bressay Sound was bound to become the scene of conflict. In 1640 Dutch and Spanish fleets battled here; and in 1703 four French warships burned up to 150 busses (fishing vessels) of the fishing fleet. Fort Charlotte, built in 1668 during the Dutch wars, was burned five years later by the Dutch. Shetlanders, taking advantage of the presence of the Dutch fishermen, traded food and wool for gin, brandy, tobacco and luxuries at Hollanders Knowe, between Lerwick and Scalloway, until a settlement began at Lerwick in the early 17th century, initially as seasonal traders' shanties serving the Dutch fleet.

The esplanade looking south c.1925

Above *Queen's Hotel and the Post Office (right) from the breakwater of the small boat harbour.* Below *Post Office, seaside*

Waterfront

Before the esplanade obliterated much, Lerwick's waterfront was made up of little piers, lodberries and beaches, such as remain at the **South End**. **Victoria Pier** was built in 1886 and from then on extensions and improvements ate away at the seafront. When the pier served the 'North Boats' from Scotland and steamers to Northern Mainland and North Isles tied up at pierhead, it throbbed with life. Now the 'North Boat' makes the same entrance into Bressay Sound, but instead of sailing towards Lerwick, piled up around the harbour, it passes on to the back side of the town. Yachts, fishing fleets and the occasional liner still bring colour and vitality.

Early 20th-century buildings line the **Esplanade** including the rear of the **Post Office**, rising over the small boat harbour.

Utterly lost amongst the pierhead clutter is the diminutive, polished granite **Diana Fountain**, 1890. It commemorates the return, in 1867, of the *Diana*, a whaler from Hull, which had spent 14 months away, six of these trapped in Arctic ice; 13 crew, including nine Shetlanders, had died.

Richard Moira's 1960's **Esplanade Toilets** prompted a contemporary 'Up Helly Aa' billhead to proclaim:
*'Men and Women we may be,
But let's preserve that nicety,
And ask old Moira why the Hades,
We can't just be Gents and Ladies.'*

Finnie

Shetland Museum

Above *Old Fish Market, 1907, demolished c. 1954. Built, unusually for Shetland, in red brick, with white trim. An infill site,* built on turds and tealeaves, *the foundations gave way and its fate was inevitable*
Left *The turrets of the Grand Hotel rising over the esplanade*

Ellesmere Buildings, 1906, is a tall businesslike block thinly dressed up with string-courses and scrolled pediments. In a rather belated sentiment, a medallion of Queen Victoria graces the pediment of **Victoria Buildings**, 4 1905. The **Harbour Master's Office**, 1906, is a rather special white-painted toy-box, with turn-of-the-century curved dormerheads and proportions.

Leask's, *c.*1900, John M Aitken
The harbourfront end of **90 Commercial Street**, higher here and better for it, was the office of the grandly titled North of Scotland, Orkney & Shetland Steam Navigation Co. A painted stone plaque over the door commemorates the *Sovereign*, a paddle-steamer which set up a regular Shetland run in 1836 — not, however, by the N of S, O & S Co. The **Peerie Shop**, between Greig's Closs and Campbell's Closs, a lodberry, *c.*1735, once on the waterfront at Greig's pier, was restored by 5 Richard Gibson in 1987. **Albert Buildings**, *c.* 1900, restored 1990, Richard Gibson. A two-storey timber shed clad in red corrugated sheet and with an outpost-of-the-empire look. The first floor external walkway was used for net drying.

The **Esplanade** merges into **Commercial Road** leading north. Landward, bordering the New Town's edge, are tenements over shops. The seaward side borders an extensive area of former fishing stations, now harbouring small

The esplanade in the herring days, c.1925 — Albert Buildings centre

Shetland Museum

businesses as well as decay. There is scope for sensitive development. **North Ness House**, c.1820, is a solid former farmhouse marooned in industry. **Malakoff**, a boatyard since the 19th century, has tall ironclad premises. An ironclad two-storey gutters hut from the heyday of herring survives on the North Ness. Its external walkway is intact but its future uncertain.

Hay's dock and storehouse shell, given over to pleasure boats

6 **Hay's Dock**, 19th century
Stone-built, silted and used by small craft: with great unrealised potential, as has the roofless storehouse. Other relics of Hay & Co's trading past remain in substantial warehouses. **Skipidock** is similar. **Holmsgarth Road** runs over the sites of herring stations with much reclaimed land and commercial docks.

P & O Ferry Terminal, 1976,
Leslie D Morrison & Partners
Dismal travel aesthetics in a harled and lead-clad package. No romance of the sea here; only the prefabricated, stacked boxes of the **Shetland Hotel**, 1982, await the traveller.

North Road Housing, 1988, Richard Gibson
This development brings the scale of the dense lanes of Lerwick to a steep site, with parallel terraces of housing stepping down the slope. Particularly good landscaping. A few fish-gutters' huts from the herring days, mostly reclad, remain on North Road.

Above *A survivor, herring boom gutters hut at Gremista.* Left *The Böd of Gremista*

7 **Böd of Gremista**, late 18th century
This tall harled house, its windows protected by external shutters, standing rather forlorn amongst desolate pipeyards, was the birthplace of Arthur Anderson, whose father was in charge of fish-curing at Gremista. The böd (booth) had storage in the ground floor with the family living above. *Museum, summer opening; guide book available.* Oil rig service bases from the 1970s stretch northwards.

Dales Voe Oil Rig Base, 1986,
Archibald Henderson & Partners, Engineers
Massive steel hangars developed beside deep water to allow rigs to come alongside for servicing. The Administration Building by Richard Gibson is slick and businesslike, clad in white panels. **Kebister**, just beyond the boundary fence, has revealed to excavation Iron Age Houses and the store-house of Henry Phankouth, Archdeacon of Shetland, *c.*1500.

Lerwick Lanes

Lerwick and Bressay Sound drawn by John Irvine c.1840. Looking north, St Olaf's Hall centre with St Columbas to the right and Greenfield House with tower

8 **Whitegates**, 1954, Richard Moira
A sculpted form, stark white walls being

23

Above *Whitegates*. Right *2 and 4 Greenfield Place*. Below *The tower added to St Magnus Episcopal Church in 1891*

Lanes (Closes)

A network of lanes clambers from Commercial Street to the ridge above and, for a long time, were the slums of Lerwick. In the early 1970s, large areas were demolished and only now is the locality being re-evaluated. Most lanes, generally called closses, were named from their first developers. In 1845, the Police Commissioners replaced their early names by ones from contemporary political events — Pitt, Fox and Reform — as well as from Sir Walter Scott's fiction — Pirate and Norna.

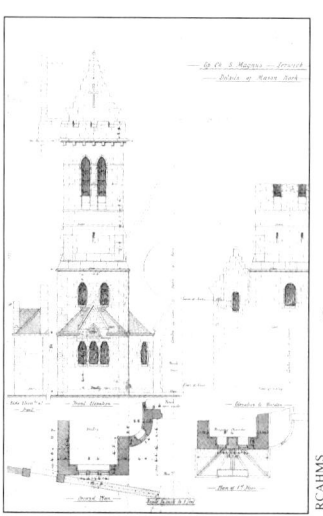

anchored by prominent chimney stacks, one black, one blood red.

St Magnus Episcopal Church,

Greenfield Place, 1862-4, Alexander Ellis
The gabled front end reflects the straightforward nave and chancel behind. Ellis, architect of a series of Aberdeen churches, (see **Aberdeen** and **Banff and Buchan** in this series) added the gutsy battlemented tower in 1891. Windows by Sir Ninian Comper were moved here in 1973 from the chapel of the former House of Charity in Knab Road. Their restraint contrasts with earlier, harsher glass. Notice the tiny strawberries on two of Comper's windows — in memory of his father who died in Aberdeen's Duthie Park while giving strawberries to poor children.

Greenfield House, an odd, low cottage with dentiled eaves and a pilastered and pedimented doorway, is shown in John Irvine's view of Lerwick, *c.*1840, with a central clock tower. **2 and 4 Greenfield Place** are solid 18th century. Where **Church Road** has sliced through the lanes, ragged edges remain. **Bonavista**, 26 Church Lane, and the only remains of that lane, is a grander town house built for Bruce of Symbister (Whalsay) in the early 19th century, with two storeys and garret over a basement.

9 St Columba's, 1825-9

Lerwick's Parish Church is cool, severe Georgian. Full-width steps to three identical wide doors and broad windows above. The only details are string-courses and mouldings around openings. The interior and apse are Victorian. The growth of Lerwick had justified its becoming a separate parish from 1701. A church had been built *c.*1660 and a larger one built around it in 1783, which, since altered, remains as the Masonic Hall in Queen's Lane.

St Olaf's Hall, 1849, was the Free Church, a plain hall decorated with Gothic pinnacles.

Annsbrae House, 1791

Built on a site originally called 'Hungryhaa', this town residence of Mouat of Garth brought 'polite' architecture to Lerwick. Fronted by a formal garden, the main two-storey harled block is flanked by low offices. Impeccably restored as housing by Shetland Island Council architects in 1987. A new rear block continues the rustic classicism with a colonnade.

Heddel's Park, Gardie Lane/Mounthooly Place, 1956, Richard Moira

The best of Moira's infills, unassuming houses, stepping up and along the contours with robust

Left *Annsbrae, prior to restoration.* Top *Law Lane.* Above *Looking down Pitt Lane.* Below *Heddels Park Housing*

hard landscape. Still notably fresh. A huge chunk of the area between **Pitt Lane** and **Hill Lane** was torn out and replaced by the soulless box of **Lerwick Swimming Pool**, 1972, Zetland County Architects, in a sea of car parking. Pitt Lane was redeveloped with council houses in 1984.

10 **John Jamieson's Closs**, Hill Lane, 1982, Richard Gibson
Twin-gabled housing blocks, an intimate closs between set across the the dominating lane pattern. Crisp stark white harling.

New Town
Lerwick's New Town was born of necessity. The overcrowded lanes offered no land for building. In 1862 Ross Smith, a watchmaker, wrote to the

Top *John Jamieson's Closs*. Above *St Olaf Street and the Town Hall rising over*

'Parties obtaining feus should be at liberty to put up erections of such elevations and of such styles of architecture as they may see fit, provided they keep the line of street and do not build with the gable to the street as has been done to such an extent in the present time.'
Shetland Advertiser, 23 March 1863

Shetland motto on No. 64 St Olaf Street, dated 1886

editor of the *Shetland Advertiser*: 'Are we not to get a proper ground plan of the town property, providing for the further drainage and sewerage of a probable town to be built, with proper frontages, wide streets and airy lanes?' On 7 May the Feuars and Heritors called for a layout to be prepared on the town park's area from Roderick Coyne of Edinburgh. Development was slow and concentrated on the **Scalloway Road** and **Burgh Road** area. The impetus was revived in 1878 when a revised layout was prepared, with two north/south streets crossed by four minor streets. The principal street was to be 50ft wide and the rest 40ft. In the 1880s, the herring fishing had begun to boom and there was now no holding back the building of villas. An earlier street, **High Street**, ran diagonally from the Hillhead to Commercial Road until it was 'rationalised' to the regular grid to become **St Olaf Street**.

11 **Town Hall**, 1884, Alexander Ross
Gothic Baronial, from the architect of Inverness

Finnie

The **Town Hall** (*left* – original drawing showing spire) was supposedly built back to front, facing away from rather than towards the harbour. Although the northern part of the New Town had not at that time been laid out it seems appropriate to have faced the building towards the new area rather than to the old lanes.

Finnie

Cathedral, rising high above the town like some Flemish cloth hall. Its expresses the confidence of the burghers and the subscribers who paid £2 for each of 2000 shares. Ross's first plans show the building surmounted by a flèche. John M Aitken, the contractor, is said to have suggested the rather alien and clumsy tower, the £400 for which was presented by a group of subscribers. Much heraldry on the exterior, and even more within. The entrance hall has armorial panels from the principal Scottish cities and towns with which Shetland had connections. Civic pride reaches its zenith in the first-floor hall glowing with the strong colours of stained glass featuring historical characters from the island's history including Margaret, Princess of Denmark.

Lystina House, 1885
A smart, gabled, villa built, for the merchant George R Tait, in Aberdeen bond using granite from the island of Hildasay. Erected, it is said, to cover the embarrassment of a back-to-front Town Hall.

Finnie

Left *Alexander Ross's drawing for the Town Hall — with spire.* Top *Town Hall and the War Memorial.* Above *County Buildings*

Zetland County Buildings & Police Station, 1875, David Rhind
One of the earliest buildings in this part of the New Town. An irregular group in a Scots domestic style made more picturesque by the many crowstepped gables. The gaol behind is

The streets owe their Scandinavian names to the revival of Nordic interest in the last quarter of the 19th century as does the symbolism of the Town Hall's stained glass and the development of Up Helly Aa in the 1880s.

The Dutch fishing fleet, from at least the 18th century, brought its own hospital and mission ship, usually named *De Hoop*. It was the custom of the parish kirk to give an 8 a.m. Sunday service to the Dutch. Wooden clogs were left in the vestibule.

suitably forbidding, a tall block pierced by small, segment-headed, windows.

War Memorial, 1923, Sir Robert Lorimer
One of Lorimer's many memorials, here in crisp white granite. An earlier design had incorporated the prow of a Viking ship but this was altered to the more conventional cross.

Shetland Museums & Library,
Lower Hillhead, 1966, Zetland County Architects
This treasurehouse of Shetland's past takes the form of a glass box floating over a splayed sandstone base. Timber panels either side of the entrance have carved knotwork and island symbols. **St Ringan's UF Church**, Lower Hillhead, 1886, by R G Sykes, is a rubbly cruciform kirk, whose gables rise up to a dumpy battlemented tower over the crossing.

Top Hillhead c.1940. The gabled lane heads were one of the towns more lamentable losses. Right St Ringans. Above Methodist Manse

Adam Clarke Methodist Chapel, Hillhead, 1872, William Parslow
Adam Clarke, *c.*1762-1832, the Methodist President, took a particular interest in the promotion of Methodism in Shetland, visiting the islands on two occasions. This church to his memory by a Liverpool architect, is disappointing: a plain hall with round-headed windows on the front. The Manse, next door, *c.*1877, makes up for the church with a steep roof, tapered chimney stacks, a half-timbered bay and a porch straight out of a fairy-tale.

St Olaf Street and **King Harald Street** are the New Town's principal north/south aligned
12 streets. Between them lies **King George's Field**, sunken gardens to the southern end and a rather desolate playing field at the northern end, separated by **King Erik Street**. The northern part only comes into its own as the

burning site of the Up Helly Aa galley. In contrast with the tight spaces of the older part of Lerwick, this area is open and spacious and rather windswept.

St Clement's Hall, St Olaf Street, 1911, T L Bruce
Built to provide St Columba's with a hall and Dutch fishermen with a base to hold their services. A good rubbly gabled front and square, battlemented tower. **92 St Olaf Street**, House of David, 1905, was named after its builder, David Sutherland, a watchmaker. Three storeys of white-painted *in situ* concrete with sparse detail and a stair tower emerging curved at the top of the building. Note the vaguely turn-of-the-century parapets on **Nos 88-90**.

Islesburgh House, King Harald Street, 1907, Alexander Campbell
A striking reminder of the Great Herring Boom, built for Andrew Smith, owner of one of the largest companies in the herring trade. A wide frontage with bowed porch and window bays either side. Alexander Campbell came to Lerwick as Clerk of Works on the Town Hall and stayed, becoming burgh surveyor. One of the many New Town houses built by John M Aitken.

Throughout the New Town, magnificent railings have survived time and Second World War Weapons Appeals for scrap metal. Florid Victorian examples co-exist with some wonderful, sinuous, turn-of-the-century metalwork.

13 **Isleburgh Community Centre**,
King Harald Street, 1902, John M Aitken
The former Central Public School, its tall front distinguished by Aitken's pepperpots and crowsteps. The architect's obituary in 1923 stated: *'There is no finer public school in the north of Scotland — either as to internal arrangements or architectural beauty.'*

Top *Railings, New Town.* Middle *House of David, 92 St Olaf Street.* Bottom *St Clement's Hall.* Left *Islesburgh House*

Above *Islesburgh Community Centre.* Below *John M Aitken's letterheading displaying his most prestigious jobs*

John Morgan Aitken, 1852-1923
'As a fact, all the public buildings which go to promote the beauty and utility of Lerwick, are the result of his skill and handiwork.' After learning his trade in Edinburgh, Aitken set himself up as a builder and architect, in Lerwick, in 1873 when the herring boom was just about to begin. His first major building contract was the Town Hall; and business boomed thereafter, with a job list running to over 140 buildings, including lighthouses on Sule Skerry and the Bass Rock. Below — his letterhead.

32-36 King Harald Street, 1885,
John M Aitken
No 32, **Summerside House**, Aitken's own home curiously displays none of his distinctive details. The short terrace has mansard roofs and segment-headed windows instead. No **32** is slightly larger than the others with some carved detail: JMA and the date appear in a florid cartouche on the end gable.

Scalloway Road, the main road south, consists of villas, council houses and a few bungalows. **Harbour Street** is the only east/west street of the New Town to penetrate as far as the harbour. The streets north, between Harbour Street and Commercial Road, are more artisan with smaller plots and houses.

St Margaret's RC Church, Harbour Street, 1911, James M Baikie, Kirkwall
This neat kirk of buttressed nave and apse is built of Bressay freestone with facings of Eday stone. A large stained-glass window was inserted in the east gable in 1986; the design, illustrating Shetland scenes and themes, is disrupted by mullions. More crenellations on the 14 **Excelsior Bar**. **Brentham Place**, 1900, by Alexander Campbell, with its wealth of Baronial detail is one of the best commercial buildings in the town.

For all its benefits, the New Town had done little to relieve the overcrowding and conditions of the poor in the lanes, — until the construction of the tenements at Nos **7-13, St Magnus Street**, *c.*1909, put up by the feuars and heritors of the burgh to help alleviate the housing shortage. **Garrison Theatre**, Market Street, is

faced by a domestic front, 1903, all crowsteps and a dumpy tower.

15 **Burgh Road**: *'all the way up Burgh Road nothing used to be heard but the grunting of pigs. Now there was nothing but the tinkling of pianos.'* Formerly the outer edge of the burgh and one of the first areas of the New Town to be developed, decent villas line the east side until merging into tenements nearer Commercial Road. Burgh Road remained the town's boundary until 1938. Post-war housing now stretches to **Clickimin Loch** with a few 19th-century properties in its midst.

16 **The Knab**
The town's central ridge, forming a headland dominating the south approach to Bressay Sound, was the location of Second World War defences. **Coastguard Station**, 1986, PSA Architects, dominates the summit. Overscaled and sculptural it is best read, as intended, from a distance. At Twageos Road, Coastguard houses occupy the site of 18th century Twageos House, demolished in 1961. Much of the rest of the Knab is occupied by the **Anderson High School** complex, centred on the **Anderson Institute**, 1860, Arthur Anderson's major gift to Shetland. A sprawling Scottish mansion by *'an architect from Aberdeen'*, with square and octagonal towers, and a Gothic traceried oriel window. Hammerbeam roof in the Library.

Altogether different is the **Bruce Hostel**, dated 1919, although work had began in 1914 and was not completed until 1923. Gifted by Robert Bruce of Sumburgh and designed by W Laidlaw

Arthur Anderson, 1792-1868
Born at Gremista, he worked as a beachboy — curing and drying fish — on Bressay. His initiative was noticed by the factor, Thomas Bolt, who helped Arthur obtain a position in the Royal Navy. After Napoleon's defeat and Anderson's discharge, he was employed by, and became partner of, Brodie McGhie Willcox. Together they set up a shipping business with Spain and Portugal. Successful, expanding and winning postal contracts they became the Peninsular & Oriental Steam Navigation Company — P & O. The Shetland link remains. Anderson, concerned for the conditions of the Shetland people, served as Member of Parliament for Orkney and Shetland from 1847 to 1852. He founded the island's first newspaper, set up an independent fishing station and was largely responsible for Shetland being served by a regular mail-boat. **Anderson High School's motto** *'Doe weel and persevere'* were the parting words of Thomas Bolt when Arthur Anderson set off, in 1808, to volunteer for the Royal Navy.

Left *Hayfield House, c.1820, a merchant's villa, now council offices, marooned amidst council houses with its leafy policies in decay.* Below *Twageos House*

Shetland Library

Finnie

Top *Anderson Institute.* Above
Coastguard Station

Macdougall, estate agent at Sumburgh, and W
W Reid, later to be burgh surveyor. The frontage
is loosely baroque possible influenced by
Burnet's Bank of Scotland where, as here, John
M Aitken was contractor. Aitken was certainly
responsible for the design of the massive
perimeter walls with their drum piers and
lancet decoration.

Janet Courtney Hostel, 1939, James Shearer
of Dunfermline
A modernistic block, for the Carnegie United
Kingdom Trust, with overlapping planes. The
stairs are emphasised by a tall sculpted grid of
windows. The **Lighthouse Buildings**, off Knab
Road, have prominent parapeted gables, white
render and the usual tall chimney stacks on this
block of houses. **Glen Orchy**, Knab Road,
*c.*1903, the former House of Charity, (a daughter
house of St Margaret's Convent, Aberdeen) lost
the windows from its chapel to St Magnus
Episcopal Church. **Knab Road and Breiwick
Road** comprise 120 council houses completed in
1923 in Garden City style and layout.

Finnie

Janet Courtney Hostel

Clickimin and Sound

Finnie

17 Clickimin Sports Centre, 1985,
Faulkner-Brown, Hendy Watkinson Stonor
Enviable, oil-funded facilities, compactly
packaged under a massive red metal roof with
comparatively low walls around. It hugs the
ground like a giant turtle.

Clickimin Sports Centre and Lerwick

Finnie

Left *Clickimin Broch.* Below
*Clickimin Broch drawn by Sir Henry
Dryden c.1860*

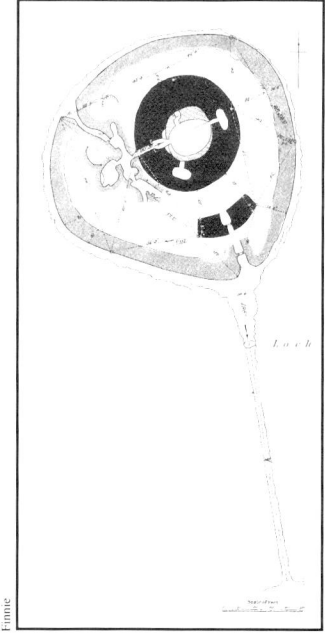

18 Clickimin Broch
The Loch of Clickimin has at various periods
been tidal, and its water level changed. Lerwick
has encroached, and development now fringes
the loch on three sides. Occupying an islet (now
joined to the shore by a causeway) is not only a
broch but a whole series of structures dating
back to a Late Bronze Age farmstead c.700-
500BC. The complex development of the site is
covered in detail by the exemplary guide book
which includes Mousa. A Bronze and Early Iron
Age farmstead was developed into an Iron Age
fort with a drystone ring wall around the islet
and a strong blockhouse at the entrance. It is
thought that these supported lean-to ranges of

Finnie

33

Top *Clickimin Broch drawn by Sir Henry Dryden c.1860.* Middle *Interior of Clickimin Broch.* Bottom *Clickimin Broch.* Below *Westhall*

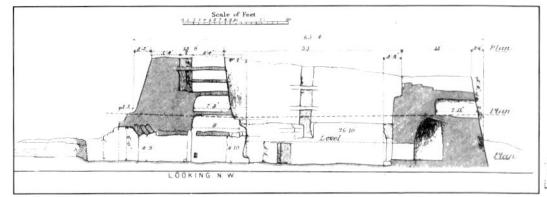

'The summer residencies of Mr Hay, Mr Ogilvy, Mr Greig and Mr Duncan display, on a limited scale, such as the locality admits of, considerable taste and spirit of improvement.' **Westhall**, *c.*1840, the residence, originally, of Mr Greig, procurator fiscal, is a rather dull brown rendered house with a wide pediment and glazed-in porch. Mr Ogilvy's house, **Seafield**, *c.*1840, is elegant Georgian, in ashlar with parapets and gently bowed bays. The stable block has a central arched opening with a pyramid-roofed doocot above. **Helendale**, later 19th century, retains its tree plantation.

timber accommodation around the inner face. The blockhouse, still impressive at one storey high, originally rose to three. When the loch, blocked by a spit, became no longer tidal, its level rose and a landing stage was built. To provide more accommodation, an inner ring wall was begun. Never completed, it was built over when a new wave of southern immigrants brought the technique of broch building. The broch was 19.8m (65ft) in diameter and rose probably to 12-15m (40-50ft); Mousa is 15m (50ft) wide and 13.3m (43ft) high. The broch has two entrances, one at ground level and one at first-floor level and although much reduced, it is still impressive, particularly internally. More settled conditions made defence unnecessary, and the tower was partly demolished and a wheelhouse erected within. At the end of the wheelhouse period, the settlement was abandoned and not reoccupied during the Viking or medieval periods. On the causeway a stone can be seen bearing the impression of two footprints.

Shetland Museum

Sound

'Sound was Sound when Lerwick was nane,'
according to an old saying. Now Lerwick has
engulfed the crofting township and housing
sprawls upwards and onwards. No worse nor
better than elsewhere, it draws attention to how
much is concealed by trees in more southern
latitudes. The promontory of the **Ness of Sound**
rises, green and fertile, seawards. Second World
War gun emplacements remain, futuristic
structures with daring spans and cantilevers.

Sandveien, completed 1975, Richard Moira
High-density housing presenting a fortress
aspect to Clickimin. The product of political and
economic necessity, it is now undergoing an
environmental and physical rebirth. A few years
later and a world of difference, **Akrigarth**, 1982,
Moira & Wann, is a housing scheme of much
lower density with lush planting.

Sound School, 1977, Baxter Clark & Paul
Flat-roofed school extended by the same
architects in 1982 with pitched roofs, sheltering
screen walls and projecting windows. The best,
amid all the housing sprawl, is **Sandy Loch
Water Treatment Works**, 1979, Consarc
Partnership, Architects; entirely appropriate in
the Shetland landscape, with its harled walls
and grey, pitched, roofs.

Finnie

Top *A contemporary photograph of
the township of Sound looking
towards Lerwick.* Above *Sandveien*

Finnie

Sandy Loch Waters Works

Above *The round towered St Magnus, Tingwall Kirk drawn by William Aberdeen in the 18th century. Right Tingwall Kirk and Burial Aisle, the remains of the earlier St Magnus*

Shetland Archives

CENTRAL MAINLAND

Long voes run from the south-west deep inland continued by valleys. Being composed of limestone, the district provides some of the county's best agricultural land.

Tingwall

The fertile Tingwall valley, which crosses the country, is central to island communications: Here leading Norsemen gathered, and the site of their parliament, the Lawting, survives on a secure islet at the north of Tingwall Loch, connected to the shore by a causeway over boggy ground. Delegates set up camp in the surrounding valley.

Finnie

The medieval St Magnus Church, demolished in 1788, was one of three round-towered medieval churches (similar to St Magnus on the Orkney island of Egilsay) which, by tradition, were gifted by three Norse sisters: the eldest gave St Magnus to Tingwall, the middle St Laurence to Burra, and the youngest St Mary to Ireland in South Mainland. St Magnus was a place of some reverence, signified by its red sandstone from Eday in Orkney being the same as that for Kirkwall's cathedral. All three churches were demolished at the end of the 18th century.'... *from a principle of barbarous economy to supply stones at a cheap rate for building the plain Presbyterian churches which now occupy their places.'*

The Revd John Turnbull, minister at Tingwall until 1867, was an agricultural improver, who experimented with sown grass and clover, introducing turnips, and persuaded crofters to build stone instead of 'feelie' (turf) dykes. His family life was tragic: at Christmas 1838 his wife, two children and a maid drowned through the ice on Tingwall loch. By 1853, only a daughter survived from eleven children.

[19] **St Magnus,** Tingwall, 1788-90
A conspicuous white-harled object, plain, oblong, and Presbyterian, with a belfry. It has a fine interior with lofts on three sides. The sole remains of the earlier church is the burial vault of the Mitchells of Westshore (Scalloway): a turf-covered mound with a moulded, arched, doorway, whose musty interior houses 17th- and 18th-century graveslabs. They include that of Andrew Crawford, Master of Works to the Earl of Orkney, responsible for the Earl's Palace in Kirkwall, and Scalloway Castle and most likely Muness Castle. A carved 17th-century sarcophagus outside.

Of the large farms established in the Tingwall valley in the 19th century by Lerwick merchants, only Laxfirth farm remains, whilst the steading at **Veensgarth** houses a privately owned agricultural museum.

Whiteness & Weisdale
Below Wormidale hill, which commands a view

Finnie

Finnie

westwards, is **Nesbister Böd** set up by Hay & Co in 1844 on a rock at the end of a stony beach. Fish were dried on the beach before export. **Binnaness House** (Jackville), probably 19th century, is one-and-a-half storey and whitewashed, with access only by foot or sea (a good reason for its use as a wireless station for the 'Shetland Bus'). **St Ola's Kirk**, Whiteness, 1837, tucked into a hillside beside the Loch of Strom, is now a house. Of the **Castle of Strom**, perhaps as ancient as the 12th century, only walls now remain on an islet in the loch. **Whiteness School**, 1976, Baxter Clark & Paul, is low and boxy with a Nordic design on an external wall. **Soundside**, an unremarkable but colourful voeside settlement, is Scandinavian when observed from high from the opposite side of the voe. **Huxter**, a plain house (formerly an inn at the half-way point between Walls and Lerwick in the last century), huddles behind a small plantation of trees. Scant remains of **Our Lady's Kirk** in the waterside graveyard at Soond; a place of pilgrimage in medieval times. Here, sheltered trees grow amid the remains of a house of some quality which was the birthplace of John Clunies Ross.

The *Standing Stone* on the roadside heading west is a recent replacement of the original Sojer's Stane (lost during roadworks!), commemorating roadbuilding by soldiers in the late 18th century. The monolith (above) between Tingwall and Asta lochs is said to mark the site of the slaughter in 1389 of Malisa Spere and seven of his followers by Henry St Clair, Earl of Rosslyn after a quarrel at a Ting over possession of the Earldom.

King of the Cocos Islands, John Clunies Ross, was born at Soond in 1786, and went to sea. He visited and, in 1827, settled on Direction Island in the Indian Ocean, where he became self-appointed ruler.

Top Left *Nesbister Böd*. Bottom Left *The former St Ola's Whiteness with the remains of the Castle of Strom on its islet*. Below *Weisdale Mill*

Finnie

Weisdale Church, 1863
Formerly the Free Kirk, this plain harled box is

Finnie

The hated **David Dakers Black** from Brechin bought land in the Weisdale valley from Charles Ogilvy in 1843 and immediately began a swift, cruel policy of evicting tenants in order to form a model, improved, farm. From the stones of the Northouse crofts, Kergord (then Flemington) House was built. In a short time around 300 people had left. Black was to continue his policy throughout Weisdale with his acquisition, in the 1850s, of lands from Scott of Scalloway and the Earl of Zetland.

relieved by dressed stone pinnacles at the corners and a peaked belfry. The **Kergord valley** continues inland from Weisdale Voe. In the 1850s the valley was cleared and it is now empty, although lush with established tree plantations. The rubble **Weisdale Mill**, 1855, was once Shetland's largest grain mill. It is subject to 1987 competition winning proposals, by Richard Gibson, for conversion to an Arts and Crafts centre.

Kergord House

Kergord House, *c.*1850
White-painted with black bands and details. The walled park was planted in the 1920s with a variety of tree species, creating an atmosphere redolent of Scotland's west coast. The house served during the Second World War as administrative HQ for the 'Shetland Bus'. Lonely **Sandwater**, a '*wayside public house*' in the last century, was the site of livestock roups.

Floki Vilgerdarson who nearly became Iceland's first permanent settler (returned instead to Norway) passed through Shetland in 865 on his way to Iceland. One of his daughters Geirhilda, drowned here giving her name to Girlsta Loch. In this loch Arctic Char, stranded after the Ice Age, developed into their own unique race, the Slender Char.

21 On the east coast of Mainland, **Girlsta Mill**, 1861, is another commercial mill (its vertical wheel intact), erected by Hay & Co, Lerwick merchants. Kiln and granary are integral, the kiln indicated by the roof-vent. Nearby, a large lime-kiln, again by Hay's, 1870, to cash in on the demand for lime in Lerwick's New Town.

Laxfirth House, from 18th century
The present two storey, five bay, harled house with stone dressings, under a hipped slated roof is probably an 1840 recasting of an earlier house.

Lime Kiln at Girlsta

SCALLOWAY

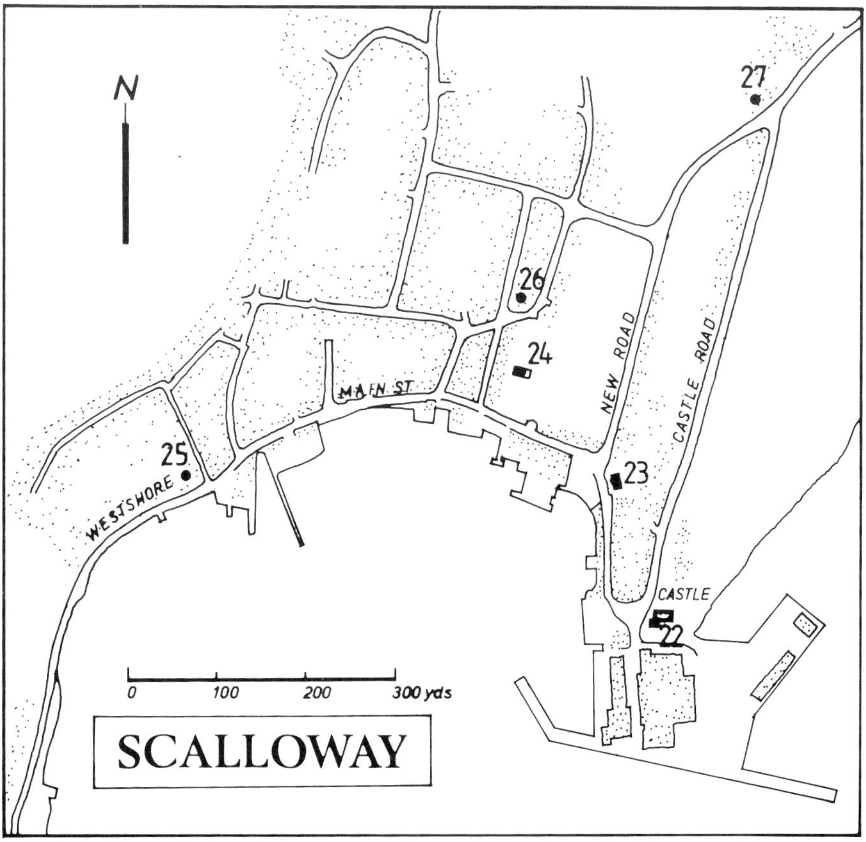

SCALLOWAY

*'The principal town is Scola Vo (Scalloway), of
about 100 poor houses and one pretty stone house
of the King's where the Governor resides.'*
Edward Montagu, 1665

RCAHM

Blacksness, Scalloway, photographed in 1971 before pier expansion

Earl Patrick Stewart succeeded his father as Earl of Orkney and Lord of Shetland in 1593. The Stewarts enforced a change from Norse to Scots rule, and the lawting was moved from Tingwall to Scalloway. Minor offences were punished with harsh penalties and confiscation of property, through which they amassed wealth and estates. The unrest which followed led to Earl Patrick's arrest in 1609. The insurrection in Orkney raised by his son Robert was unsuccessful and both men were executed in Edinburgh in 1615. Whilst deservedly unpopular, Patrick did not fill his court with Scots favourites: the names of underfoudes (bailies) remained Norse. Perhaps more damaging to ordinary folk were the clergy and hangers-on who, even after the demise of the Stewart dynasty, built up estates and fortunes.

The name of Shetland's largest village (or second town) is possibly from the Norse: *Skalavagr* — Bay of the Skali (hall). Scalloway sits at the southern end of the Tingwall Valley, on the great bay which bites into Mainland's south-west coast, sheltered by islands. Shetland's ancient capital and seat of Earl Patrick Stewart, Scalloway was prosperous until the town of Lerwick's emergence in the 18th century. When the law courts removed to Lerwick *c*.1700, Scalloway's fortunes began to decline — although some island lairds continued to build their town houses here, notably Scott at the Haa and Mitchell at Westshore. The 19th century saw a revival in the village's fortunes as merchants replaced the lairds. They owned fishing smacks which worked banks of Foula; when these failed larger smacks exploited grounds off Faroe, Iceland and Rockall. Cod were dried on stony beaches before export. Towards the end of last century, the cod trade was replaced by a haddock and herring fishery. Now much reduced in importance, Scalloway is still largely dependent on the fluctuations of the fishing industry.

National Library of Scotland

22 **Scalloway Castle**, 1600,
Andrew Crawford, Master of Works
Marooned inland since land was reclaimed for
pier expansion, this castle still holds command
over Scalloway. Built by forced labour, it was
Earl Patrick Stewart's Shetland Renaissance
chateau and justice seat until his execution.
Thereafter a garrison for Cromwell's troops,
then decay. Tall, four-storey, oblong block with
adjoining stair tower and angle turrets aplenty,
originally harled. The entrance is in the angle
with very elaborate, but weathered, panels
above. Usual vaulted kitchens and cellars at
ground level linked by a surprisingly spacious
vaulted scale-and-platt stair to the great hall in
which traces of wall painting survived to 1703.
Turnpike stairs then led to chambers above.
Peculiar to the northern isles, chequered
corbelling, set with false shot holes between,
supports some turrets.

Professor G. Donaldson

Top *Scalloway Castle drawn in
1848, after J C Schetky.* Above
*Scalloway Castle reconstruction by
William Dodd.* Bottom *Scalloway
Castle*

Shetland Bus
With Norway under German
occupation during the Second World
War, Shetland became the base for
an operation using Norwegian
fishing boats and crew to shuttle
across the North Sea — supplying
the Norwegian underground and
returning with refugees. First set
up, by David Howarth who was
second-in-command, at remote
Lunna (East Mainland) it grew and
became more successful. Increased
back-up for repairs and servicing
was necessary and the operation
moved to Scalloway. David Howarth
was later to write the story of the
operation *The Shetland Bus*.

Finnie

The expanse of **Blackness Pier** around the castle, was built originally *c*.1830, a quay for the export of salt cod to Spain, extended in 1896 to accommodate the steamer from Leith, and again in the 1980s for the fishing fleet. **New Street**; at the southern end of this row of early cottages is a plaque by William Johnson, mason, inventor and philosopher, to explain his theories on tides and the moon. **The Bulwark** is a chunky, stone slated, rubbly booth at sea level.

Above *Gibblestone House before restoration*. Right *Scalloway Haa*

23 **Old Haa of Scalloway**, *c*.1750

A tall, plain haa, three storeys of five bays, dilapidated but bold. The finely moulded doorway has an armorial panel commemorating the marriage in 1750 of James Scott to Katherine Sinclair, heiress of estates in Scalloway and Houss (Burra). Now converted to flats.

Main Street hugs a partly reclaimed shoreline. Reminders of a past prosperity survive in former businesses and the hotel. **Scalloway Museum** houses a cosy local interest collection, including much on the 'Shetland Bus'.

Haas are the houses of gentry or prosperous merchants from the 17th century onward. Originally two-storey, thick-walled, houses with irregular smallish windows, the form developed into taller, more regular, houses, reaching its peak *c*.1735 when large numbers were built. The form continued well into the 1800s, incorporating Georgian features along the way. They are unusually tall buildings for such windswept islands. Scots immigrants, who rapidly became the landowning class, would have brought their own tradition of lairds' tall houses, and the expense and difficulties of importing lengths of timber would necessitate the short spans between walls and the smallest possible roof area.

24 **Gibblestone House**, late 18th century

Fashionable town house with symmetrical wings, later pilastered porch and bay windows. The Scotts, prospering, removed from their Haa and named their new mansion after their ancestral estate of Gibliston in Fife. Ground in front led to a pier, now swallowed up by the seafront swimming pool. The house has been converted, 1989, Richard Gibson, into flats with houses set, symmetrically, into the grounds. Last survivor of seven kippering kilns which operated from the 1850s, preserving fish for export, the **Kiln Bar** retains its tall vented roof. **Dinapore**, early 20th century, erected by local Indian Doctor D'Silva, is topped by a crenellated parapet. It was used as the 'Shetland Bus' HQ.

Church of Scotland, 1840
A severe plain box with hipped roof and a tiny belfry over the frontage staring out to sea. The interior has a horseshoe gallery on fluted columns. **Scalloway Methodist Church**, 1861, is small, simple but elegant, the gable tapering into belfry. **Prince Olav Slipway**, 1942, was built to repair Norwegian fishing vessels used for the 'Shetland Bus'. Norwegian sailors were housed in what is now **Westshore Garage**, a former sail loft, looking suitably Scandinavian in rusty-red corrugated iron. The **house**, dated 1906, on the corner of Main street and Hillside Road, has a refined, chamfered, corner.

25 **Westshore**
Only scant vestiges remain within the walled garden of the mansion of Mitchell of Westshore. Today, as in 1774, the trees are notable. *'the garden, tho' small, seems the best wooded of any I had yet seen in these isles, the trees growing much above the walls, which is not often the case either here or in Orkney.'* G Low. Beyond, straggly development to **Port Arthur**. Here is the site for the **North Atlantic Fisheries College** due for completion in 1992 to designs by Forgan and Stewart. Remains of Second World War gun emplacements.

26 **Scalloway Village Hall**, 1902
A gloriously confident Edwardian building, packed with period details: pedimented gable over an attenuated Venetian window, crowsteps, a castellated round tower and some Free Style stonework at the entrance. All topped by a stumpy clock tower. Attractive interior with an open timber roof.

Top *Seaward front of the Church of Scotland, Scalloway.* Above *Scalloway Public Hall*

27 **Scalloway Junior Secondary School**, 1876, the major part 1985, Shetland Islands Council
A horizontal block under an oversailing hipped roof. Fashionable gridded glazing. **Games Hall**, 1988, by the same architects, white-rendered walls crushed under a lumbering mass of tiled roof.

Scalloway School

SOUTH MAINLAND

Most settlements and the road, in the long leg of Shetland stretching south to Sumburgh Head, follow the east coast.

Gulberwick

A broad amphitheatre overlooking Gulber Wick, now becoming a dormitory of Lerwick with a confident little **church** of 1897. It was probably hereabouts that Earl Rognvald and Earl Harald were shipwrecked in *c.*1150 on their return to Orkney after spending the summer in Norway as guests of the King. **Hollanders Knowe**, where Shetlanders traded with the Dutch Herring fleet before Lerwick was founded, lies inland marked by a small memorial stone.

Thomas Telford's Quarff Kirk

28 **Quarff Church of Scotland**, 1828, Thomas Telford

This *'ideal building'* is one of the 42 Parliamentary churches provided by an Act of Parliament of 1823 to meet deficiencies in the Highlands and Islands. Standard T-plan Telford design with a cavernous interior. **Roseville**, *c.*1830, Telford's single-storey manse, has been sadly mutilated.

Fladdabister is a township of great character. Most houses, now roofless, are beautifully built of thin bedded stone. Two beehive **Limekilns**, in use until the 1930s, burned alternative layers of limestone and peat.

Catpund Burn has steatite (soapstone) workings visible in the stream bed and on outcrops. Soapstone, a soft rock and greasy to touch, was worked into utensils in ancient times: the Norse exported pots to Iceland and Orkney.

29 **Cunningsburgh** is an area of crofting townships with the community facilities strung along the roadside. The **Public Hall**, 1987, by Phil Dean & Jan Jessop, is a stylish and economical design, neatly contained under a

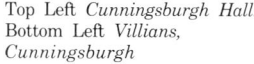

Top Left *Cunningsburgh Hall.*
Bottom Left *Villians,*
Cunningsburgh

Isolation has probably saved Mousa from being plundered for building stone. On at least two occasions the broch has given refuge. *Egil's Saga* relates how an eloping couple were shipwrecked on their way from Norway to Iceland and took refuge in Moseyjarborg. Similarly the *Orkneyinga Saga* tells how, in 1153, Erlend abducted Margaret, mother of Earl Harald Maddadson, from Orkney to Shetland and established themselves here. Harald followed and besieged the broch but happily there was a reconciliation and Erlend and Margaret were married.

green metal roof. The 1977 **Primary School** by Baxter Clark & Paul is flat-roofed with an external panel of stylised Norse galleys. The former **Manse** at Mail, *c.*1844, is plain, elegant Georgian with a steep piended roof. Aloof, it dominates the little disused church. The **Kirkyard** at Mail is ancient, as witness runic stones found here. Nearby, **Villians**, a particularly picturesque croft-house, retains thatched outbuildings.

Left *Mousa Broch.* Below *Mousa Broch, the shell of the Haa behind. Traces of outer works around the broch can be seen*

30 **Mousa Broch**, *c.*1st century *BC* — 1st century *AD*
Surpasses all other brochs. There is much power in this apparently simple form. Massive hollow

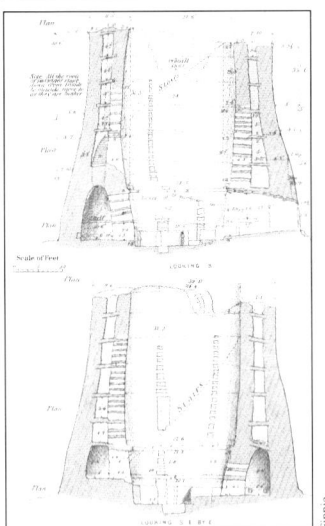

Above *Mousa Broch, after a drawing by Sir Henry Dryden in 1861.* Right *Mousa Broch, from a drawing by G Low in 1774.* Bottom Right *Leebotten, Sand Lodge and copper workings in the background and the island of Mousa beyond.* Below *Sand Lodge*

walls rise to over 13m (42ft), probably little short of the original height. The distinctive, elegant pepperpot form tapers from 15m (49ft) diameter at the base to 12m (39ft) at the parapet. Access is by a low passageway through to the central court. Three cells occupy the wall thickness with six gallery levels above; the stair cuts through to reach the parapet. There are curious, ladderlike, tiers of openings to the court. Former lean-to accommodation within the broch is indicated by stone scarcements which supported the tiered timber structures. Beyond the broch lies the shell of Mousa's **Haa**, built by the Pypers in the late 18th century, and eastwards the extensive ruins of a crofthouse and its outbuildings including a kiln.
Access to Mousa by prearranged ferry; guidebook available

31 **Sandwick** covers a large, south-east-facing area: older settlements at Leebotten and Hoswick, elsewhere oil-era housing schemes spread over open hillsides.

Sand Lodge, possibly from 17th century Long used by the Bruces of Sumburgh as a half-way house between their various properties before John Bruce bought the Sandwick estate *c.*1770. The rear wing is oldest. Several phases of additions culminate in an Edwardian smoking room, suitably lined in dark timber. At some time the old house was given parapets, with an unusual use of red brick for eaves and string-courses. All is unified by grey render. In front of the entrance are a 1789 pedestal sundial and a doocot. Copper-mines here operated intermittently from 1798 until the 1870s and the terrace of low cottages at Leebotten housed miners. The extensive remains of **Burraland Broch** sit opposite Mousa Broch, the two guarding the southern approach into Mousa Sound.

Sandwick Church of Scotland, 1807

Plain and harled, the little belfry was added in 1897 and its good timber-lined interior two years later. The kirkyard has an enclosure containing memorials to the Bruces of Sand Lodge, with anthemion-decorated iron gates. An early kirk is indicated by mounds. The **Manse**, *c.*1830, Thomas Telford, another single-storey parliamentary model (as Quarff), but intact.
Sandwick Junior Secondary School, 1984, Shetland Islands Council Architects, is a large complex, low harled buildings spread over the gently sloping site.

Hoswick Case
In 1888, the fishermen of Hoswick drove 300 whales ashore and resisted when several local lairds claimed their share. The sheriff in Lerwick ruled that the landowners had no right to the profits. The lairds took the case to the Court of Session in Edinburgh, causing concern amongst the Hoswick men as to their costs should the case be lost. In a major victory, the decision was upheld, reversing the usual practice whereby the lairds took a proportion of the catch.

There were once hundreds of Horizontal Watermills, some remaining in use until the Second World War. Although known as Norse mills they may have earlier origins. Water enters these tiny stone structures into the lower chamber (underhouse) by a lade and timber flume (fluim). The horizontal, wooden, wheel (tirl) directly turns the upper of two millstones in the upper chamber (mealhouse). Grain is fed from a wooden hopper. Mills of this type have been named clack, or click, mills from their sound when in use, but not generally in Shetland.

Hoswick; fish curing on the beach, c.1890.

Shetland Museum

Hoswick is a cluster of former fishermen's houses, most one-and-a-half-storey. Note the tiny terraced **Maranatha and Hebron**.

Levenwick, *'in former times was much frequented by the Dutch busses (fishing boats) and smugglers'* and later by herring smacks. Levenwick is a scattered village with a splendid beach on the far side of which the circular graveyard is an early site. Levenwick **Broch** is one of the better preserved sites, with ramparts visible. At **Clumlie**, a defunct croft incorporates the remains of another broch whose walls still rise to 1.5m (5ft) with two cells visible.

Troswick ˏWater Mills, 19th century
Remains of no less than nine horizontal mills with their lades and sluices on the short length of the Burn of Clumlie. Only the lowest mill remains in working order, re-roofed in felt. Another broch mound with outer ramparts, and a bland housing estate at **Dalsetter**.
Boddam's fish-curing station was operated by Hay & Co of Lerwick; described *c.*1840 as an *'odoriferous little fishing village'*. A fishing booth with two floors, the lower storage and the upper with remains of box beds, remains at Out Voe.

RCAHMS

St Ninians Isle

32 To the west, is Bigton and **St Ninian's Isle** where, in 1958, the site, a 12th-century rectangular church over an earlier chapel, revealed a treasure trove of 28 silver objects buried below a slab around *AD*800, now in the National Museum of Antiquities in Edinburgh, although replicas may be seen in the Shetland museum. Low walls remain of the rectangular structure with an apsidal chancel. The isle joins mainland by a fine 'tombola' — an ayre of sand. One of Shetland's three medieval round-towered churches was at nearby Ireland. Towards Maywick a cottage retains its thatched roof.

Bigton House, 1788
In 1744 John Bruce married Clementine Stewart

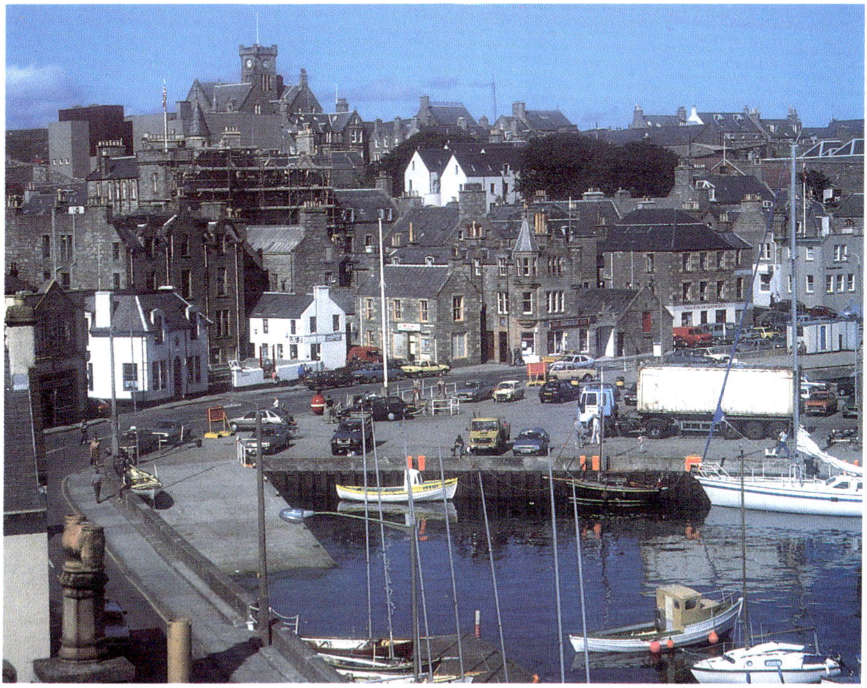

Shetland Islands Council

Finnie

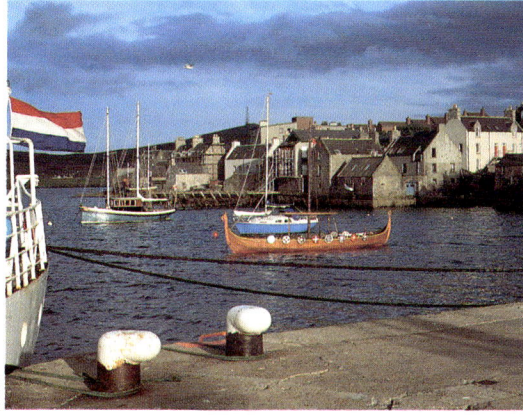

Lerwick. Top *Small boat harbour.* Above *Norse longship.* Right *Townscape for pedestrians*

Finnie

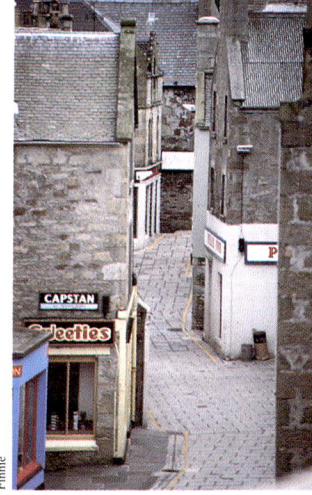

Finnie

Above *Up Helly Aa*. Right *Clickimin
Broch in the middle distance*

Finnie

Finnie

Finnie

Finnie

Left *Nesbister.* Bottom left
*Scalloway Castle, painted by
Atkinson.* Top *Weisdale.* Above
Scalloway

G D Atkinson

Finnie

Finnie

G Rowatt

Finnie

Top and above *Jarlshof*. Middle left *Fladdabister*.
Left *Indigenous construction*

Top *Sand Haa.* Above *Watermills at Leravoe.* Left *Grobsness Haa*

Top *Hillswick.* Above *Swinister Pony Pund.* Right *Dore Holm, painted by Charlton.* Below right *Voe*

Top left *Muness Castle.* Right *Belmont, Unst.* Middle left *Ham, Foula.* Right *Cullivoe.* Above *Brough Lodge*

Finnie

Finnie

National Library of Scotland

Top *Papil*. Above *Railings in
Hamnavoe*. Middle right
*Birdcatching with the Cradle of Noss
in 1774, after G. Low*. Right
*Entrance to Christie's Hole, Papa
Stour, painted by Atkinson*

G D Atkinson

Bigton House

Shetland Museum

of Bigton and replaced the house 44 years later.
His initials and the date appear above the old
entrance; he added Stewart to his name. The
main house is a two-and-a-half storey haa, the
rear wing dormered, and a Georgian porch in
the angle. In 1774 the Revd George Low found
Bigton the biggest farm in Shetland, full of bere
and oats *'both as good of their kinds as even in
the south of Scotland'*. Fields here are still large
and productive. The former **Spiggie Hotel**,
1896, is now rendered but was a timberclad
hotel for tourists and anglers.

Dunrossness (The Ness), is the southernmost
parish with Shetland's most productive
farmland. Farm buildings here have some
similarities to Orkney buildings, perhaps
resulting from the population being *'Strangers
from Scotland, and Orkney'* who presumably
brought some of their own building techniques.
Dunrossness Kirk, 1790, which replaced the
cross kirk at Quendale, is a harled rectangular
box with a little belfry. A brash modern
memorial to Betty Mouat in the kirkyard. The
Baptist Church, 1912, possibly designed by the
Revd William Fotheringham, is a rather
pretentious, rubbly, kirk with a dumpy tower
and red tiled roof.

33 **Quendale Mill**, 1867,
James Abernethy of Aberdeen, Ironfounders
Single storey mill over a laigh (lower) floor,
which retains its overshot wheel. Established as
a commercial grain mill at the time when clack
mills were going out of use. Restored, 1990, by

Betty Mouat sailed, in January
1886, from Grutness as a passenger
on the smack *Columbine* bound for
Lerwick, to sell knitwear. A heavy
sea sent the skipper overboard, and
the crew who set off in the ship's
boat to try and rescue him were
unable to return to the *Columbine*.
Betty drifted alone for eight days
before coming ashore in Lepsøy in
west Norway. Returning home via
Hull and Leith, she became
something of a celebrity.

Top *Southvoe, kiln and barn left.*
Above *Southvoe Mill*

Walter Scott
In 1814 Walter Scott accompanied
Robert Stevenson on a survey cruise
for the Commissioners of Northern
Lighthouses. It was Scott who first
named the Old House of Sumburgh
Jarlshof and set much of *The Pirate*
around it: *'a rude building of rough
stone, with nothing about it to gratify
the eye, or to excite the imagination;
a large, old-fashioned, narrow house,
with a very steep roof covered with
flags composed of grey sandstone ...
The windows were few, very small in
size, and distributed up and down
the building with utter contempt for
regularity...'*

Richard Gibson as a working museum.
Quendale House, *c.*1800, is a gaunt, late,
derelict Haa, the seat of the Griersons,
successors to the Sinclairs who, in the 17th
century, were one of Shetland's largest
landowners. In the 1670s, sand had buried much
of their land, and in the 1760s their estate went
into liquidation. The Cross Kirk *'a pretty large
church'* in 1711 stood near here. Sixty years
later the foundations were almost blown away,
and corpses were revealed in the sand, *'bones
bleached white'.*

Southvoe, *c.*1870, restored as the Shetland
Crofthouse Museum, consists of house and byre
opening either side of a cross passage and a barn
beyond, lying parallel to the main building with
a grain-drying kiln at the end. All the
paraphenalia of crofting is on display. Roofed
with straw thatch over turf: note the thatched
chimney. The associated Horizontal Mill is
rustic, toylike, and fully restored with sluices
and water lades in operation.
Open in the summer

Bruce Memorial Hall, 1909, in Edwardian
dress, was provided by the widow of John Bruce
of Sumburgh and suitably adorned with the
family arms. **Ness of Burgi Fort** is an Iron Age
fortification; a massive blockhouse with two
cells.

34 Jarlshof

Layers and layers of occupation were revealed
below the Old House of Sumburgh when gales
blew sand away in the late 19th century. Part

had been lost to the sea. The guidebook is essential in this bewilderment of occupation. Earliest was a Stone Age settlement, followed by a broch, then wheelhouse. When the Norse occupied the site, it was probably a relatively unimportant farm. Then came a medieval farmstead and, lastly, the Old House of Sumburgh. Outstanding amongst the remains are the beautifully constructed radial wheelhouses: vaulted chambers around a central space, probably roofed with a conical structure, the dwellings are surprisingly cosy. The 9th-century longhouse looks insubstantial by comparison. Topping all are the ruins of the **Old House of Sumburgh**, later 16th century, the residence of Robert Stewart who had been granted the Lordship of the Northern Isles in 1564, and tenanted by William Bruce, an immigrant Fife laird, in 1592. It was extended during a re-occupation by the Stewarts, *c.*1605.

Sumburgh Farmhouse, possibly later 17th century, was the next home of the Bruces. A tall, double pile *'old, plain, family mansion, seated in the middle of the green sward of Sumburgh.'*

51

Sumburgh House

Sumburgh Hotel, from 1867, David Rhind
The Bruces built this fashionable Baronial
mansion, whose tower is topped by a witch's cap.
Guest wings of 1897 are more rugged, with
crowsteps. Hideous bedroom additions were
added in the 1970s.

Above *Wilsness Terminal,
Sumburgh Airport.* Below
*Stevenson's elevation of Sumburgh
Light*

Sumburgh Airport, Wilsness Terminal,
1979, G R M Kennedy & Partners
Slick, modern geometric air travel international,
in dramatic contrast to its primaeval setting.
This highly visible block was erected to meet the
demands of vast increases of oil workers passing
through the airport. At Grutness a little
lighthouse service storehouse in coursed rubble,
flat roofed with hexagonal chimney stacks.

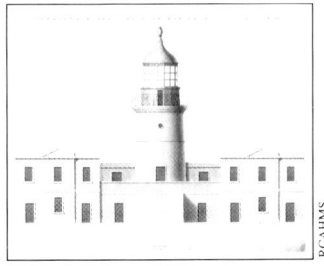

Sumburgh Head Lighthouse, 1821,
Robert Stevenson
Shetland's first lighthouse, perched high atop
Sumburgh Head at Shetland's southern tip. A
stubby tower rises from a podium between two
pedimented pavilions.

Finnie

WEST MAINLAND

Eric Linklater has described the West Mainland as '*a bewilderment of land and water*'. It covers a large, and sparsely populated, area. Spectacular coastal scenery to the west and north and a moorland interior.

Tresta is a scattered community and fairly sheltered. '*monkey puzzle and other trees*' grow here. **Store, Sandsound**, possibly from the 18th century, is a neat two-storey trader's house with a stone pier, tucked under grassy 'banks' at the sea edge. **Park Hall**, an early 20th-century curiosity built by a local doctor. *In-situ* concrete construction with cardboard-thin elevations and a pediment and pierced parapet. **Semblister Church** of 1780 replaced the chapel at Sand. A plain church, decayed, on a site more accessible by sea than land.

Finnie

Top *View over the West Mainland — Papa Stour on the horizon.* Above *Semblister Church*

Ena Tait

Park Hall. The Moorish structure (now demolished) was a septic tank cover

35 **Haa of Sand**, 1754

Almost unaltered and nearly identical to the contemporary Scalloway Haa, three storeys of five bays, one room deep. Built as his summer house by Sir Andrew Mitchell of Westshore (Scalloway) who was allegedly given leave by the Earl of Morton to remove from Scalloway Castle '*dressed freestones torn from their place to supply door and window jambs and lintels, and corner stones for this mansion*'. Two complete doorways from the castle lead into the walled policies. Moulded entrance with an armorial panel over.

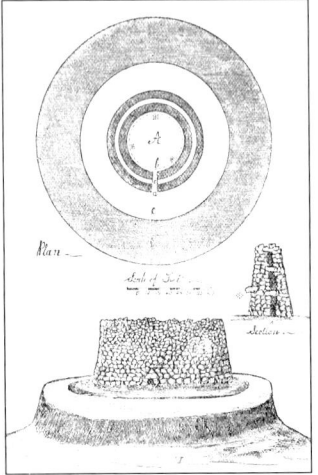

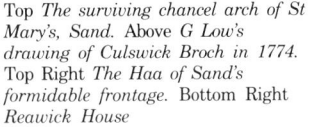

Top The surviving chancel arch of St Mary's, Sand. Above G Low's drawing of Culswick Broch in 1774. Top Right The Haa of Sand's formidable frontage. Bottom Right *Reawick House*

Reawick house was built by the Umphreys after they had acquired the Reawick estate from the Cheynes. Reawick formed part of the large Vaila Estate which the Cheynes had leased from Denmark after Gorvil Fadersdatter had resigned the estate to the Danish crown *c.*1580.

The principal rooms on the first floor and bedrooms above are panelled in Norwegian pine with mouldings, cornices and blind arcading.

St Mary's Chapel, Sand, medieval
Only the chancel arch stands of this pre-Reformation chapel, certainly pre-dating by several centuries the popular tradition that it was built by grateful survivors from an Armada shipwreck. **Reawick House**, from 1730, *'a plain, modern building of six rooms'* in 1793, looks suburban under its later red-tiled roof. Toy fort castellated-style outbuildings. **Reawick Congregational Church**, Skeld, dated 1863, has a good, white, gabled exterior, but is low inside and rather unimpressive. One must proceed from Culswick, on foot, passing **Culswick Methodist Chapel**, 1894, and idyllic, deserted, **Sotersta** with ruinous cottages, watermill and boat noosts above the 36 beach to reach **Culswick Broch**, high on a mound overlooking the entrance to Vaila Sound. Hollow walls still rise to 3m (10ft). Note the massive triangular lintel over the entrance passageway. Neolithic **Staneydale Temple**, is so much larger than other contemporary houses, that its special role as meeting house or indeed temple is assumed. The temple is a massive oval shaped structure, the wall still rising over 1.2m (4ft). Two central post holes can be seen. There

Walls, Voe House in the foreground

are many other ancient houses and field systems at Gruting and **Scord of Brouster**.

37 **Walls (Waas)** was formerly a place of some importance in the herring fishery. Although stone quays, churches and larger merchants' houses remain, and it is the centre of a large crofting area, the village has lost its former importance, and shows it.

Happyhansel School, 1982,
Shetland Islands Council Architects
Low profile in white render with a boxy, metal, hall roof rising above. Shetland's earliest school, founded in Walls in 1713 by the Society for the Propogation of Christian Knowledge, was several hundred yards up the hill, and had the same name. A Hansel was a gift — in this case of land for the school.

Bayhall, *c.*1750
The former seat of Henry of Bayhall, it is a three-storey, harled, sombre haa, three bays wide, restored and converted into flats, 1978, by Shetland Islands Council Architects and Richard Gibson. **St Paul's**, 1867, is dull Victorian. An early predecessor was a pre-Reformation chapel beside the Loch of Kirkigarth. **Voe House**, 18th century, is a two-storey, double house which, together with attached houses at each end, forms a sad, decaying, terrace. **Clubbs**, Leravoe, is a crofthouse converted by Richard Gibson

Planticrubs are found, in varied densities, throughout the islands. These small stone enclosures, around 1.5m high and 3-9m across, are generally round but often square or rectangular. They were used (many still are) to raise cabbage seedlings safe from sheep and wind. They may be built on fertile ground or have topsoil which was carried from around to increase that within.

Left *Clubbs*. Below *Bayhall*

Burrastow House

from 1973 as the architect's weekend house. The roof has been raised with a strip of glazing inserted around the old wallhead, a glass bay taking the place of the expected central porch. Two derelict horizontal watermills remain at the roadside before **Burrastow House**, 1759, now hotel. Another haa, two storeys on a raised basement, the porch reached by a fore-stair. A seat of the Henrys, the house was bought, altered, and extended, in the early part of this century by Col Foster, a Yorkshire mill-owner, as a summerhouse.

38 Island of Vaila

Granted to Robert Cheyne in 1576 by James VI *'to big ane hous and fortice upoun the saidis landis of Valay for sauftie thairof fra the hiland men, perattis, and otheris invasionis...'* Vaila passed from the Cheynes to James Mitchell of Girlsta, a Scalloway merchant. He built the Old Haa in 1696. Passing by descent to the Scotts of Melby, Vaila was sold, in 1893, to Yorkshire mill owner Herbert Anderton. Wool-buying brought him to Shetland. With his brother, he developed Vaila as a farm and the haa was expanded as the family summer residence. House parties were entertained in lavish style; fishing and shooting. (Plans to add a further wing to the house and to build a chapel to seat 100, when the island's population was 30, were abandoned *c.*1915.)

A contemporary photograph of Vaila Hall, the old Haa forming the right wing

Vaila Hall, 1696 and 1895-1900
Divided from open landscape only by its terrace, with steps guarded by stone griffins. To the old haa as the southern wing, Anderton added the parallel north wing and walled the space between for the baronial hall. All heavily castellated externally, the new wing terminates in a massive round tower, and pepperpots have corbelling in imitation of that at Scalloway and Muness Castles. St Magnus and St Rognvald, portrayed in leaded glass, flank the entrance. The Baronial hall is rich, complete with a minstrel gallery and massive fireplace and

furnished in Jacobean style with all the trappings of the house's heyday preserved *in-situ*. The old moulded entrance to the haa now leads from the hall and retains the armorial panel of the Mitchells above. Commanding the entrance to Vaila Sound, the clifftop **Lookout Tower** is two storey, reconstructed to its present Baronial form by Anderton. It was said to have been used by previous lairds to oversee their own smuggling activities, shipping in goods from French and Dutch vessels. Anderton travelled to the Far East and brought back to Vaila a Buddha and oriental artefacts with which he fitted out a **studio** in a reconstructed boathouse to become what must have been Shetland's one and only Buddhist temple (demolished). **Cloudin Farmhouse**, 1894, is a chunky square house with crowstepped gables. Four clustered chimneys emerge from the centre of the ridge influenced by Arts & Crafts styling. On the beach below the Hall remain the shells of old fishing lodges from Andersons' fishing station.

Left *The Hall, Vaila.* Above *Vaila Tower*

39 **Sandness**: '*a beautiful flat of Corn, Grass, and Meadow ground, facing the west.*' **St Margaret's Kirk**, 1792, is tiny but disused. On the east gable is a weathered stone: '*Fear God 1645*'. Some old grave slabs and 19th century wooden grave markers.

Melby House, *c.*1800
The usual haa of two storeys with a garret, and additions to the rear. **North House**, 18th century, probably preceeded Melby as the seat of the Scotts, when John, second son of John Scott of Gibliston (Fife) inherited Melby, Vaila and Foula through his mother Grizel Mitchell in 1736. Moulded skewputts are its only relief.

Arthur Anderson of P&O leased Vaila in 1837, and set up a fishing enterprise to provide a market and employment for local fishermen. He hoped to break the hold of the lairds and merchants, who made fishing a condition of tenure by their tenants. Commitments elsewhere made Anderson unable to continue and the enterprise folded, but the fishermen had had a taste of a less restrictive practice.

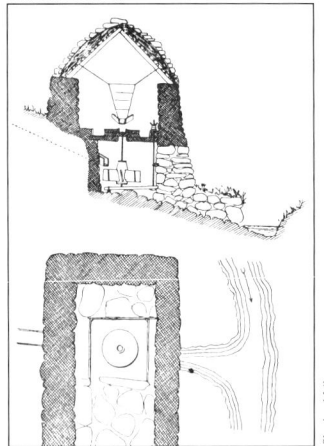

Shetland Library

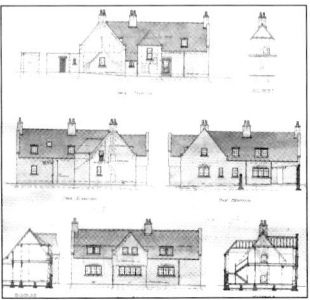

RCAHMS

Shetland Museum

Note thatched outbuildings and productive kailyards at **Huxter** where there are three horizontal **Water Mills** (the last used during the Second World War). Each sits aside the burn, served by a stone-lined lade. All have some machinery, the lowest still thatched. **Smithfield** is a thick-walled, stone-slated house with thatched barns and byres. The roadside **Kirk** at West Burrafirth has a tiny timber-lined interior and corrugated roof.

Aith expanded partly owing to expansion in the knitting industry in the 20th century, and partly from a high proportion of Aith men being employed on whaling ships. Turn-of-the-century railings front some houses. **Aith School**, 1981, by Shetland Islands Council Architects, much hipped roof evident, low site, low profile and rather low key. In **Vementry Water Mill** a roofless horizontal clack mill, some machinery remains.

40 **Vementry House**, early 1900s, possibly Sir Robert S Lorimer
Strong rectangular, two-storey, harled house, with contrasting red granite dressings and crowsteps (quarried on Vementry Isle) appendaged to an earlier crofthouse. A flat-roofed porch occupies the angle. Stylish internally with a spacious stairwell. Edmund Fraser had commissioned Lorimer to design the nearby Clousta Hotel, (destroyed by fire) and after Fraser's death in a sailing accident offshore, his two sisters had the house built. The family were neighbours of Lorimer in Edinburgh and the architect's involvement seems likely.
The **Island of Vementry** lies offshore: Shetland's best heel cairn is at Muckle Ward. The two First World War guns, still there, protected Swarbacks Minn when it was used by part of the fleet based at Scapa Flow.
Grobsness Haa, the empty hulk of a tall haa overlooks the beach in this superb spot.

Clousta Hotel (*above*, under construction), 1895, Robert S. Lorimer, (destroyed)
This was an anglers hotel. Lorimer's first design was one-and-a-half storey, harled stone with a slated roof. The remoteness and lack of local labour caused Lorimer to re-design in timber. It burned down early in this century. *Right* Vementry House — the 'Lorimer' house with quoins and crowsteps

Finnie

EAST MAINLAND

Loose, irregular coastal areas of crofts and townships straggle a splendid coastal corniche from South to North Nesting, then Laxo, Vidlin and Lunna: green voe-heads and coastline with brown heather-clad hills between. **South Nesting** is scattered. Built into the roofless ruin of a roadside cottage at **Brough** are fragments from the defunct **Old Haa of Brough**, demolished in the 1830s, including a much-weathered corbel with a carved face. Other mouldings are reused, and misused, as surrounds to door and windows.

Left *Crofting landscapes in South Nesting*. Above *Nesting Kirk*

41 **St Ola's Kirk**, North Nesting, 1794, sited next to the mound of a broch (its stone doubtless of much convenience to the church builders) is a neat box with a pavilion roof, graced by round-headed windows and an ashlar belfry. The interior is spacious and galleried. *'Exposed to all the airts of wind that blow'* is the shell of the 1770 manse at **Neap**, near its Victorian successor. **Laxo Cottage** is a tall black-and-white painted former water bailiff's house above the Laxo burn. Rather uncomfortably proportioned.

Vidlin Hall, 1913, John M Aitken, has been good, grey and gabled, but is now encumbered by later appendages. **Vidlin** clusters around its voe head, the tiny **Methodist Church** thrusts out into the water with two vertical white fins forming the belfry. **Vidlin House**, 18th century, is now much altered. Beyond Vidlin, remote Lunna Ness thrusts out into the Eastern Sea. An isthmus almost cuts the peninsula and here 42 in a haven of peace **Lunna House**, from 1660, surveys the remains of its estate. A two-storey harled and crowstepped range with a projecting wing. A crenellated bay and shallow bow windows both rise two storeys to relieve any dourness. The former seat of the Hunter family, its earliest owner was Robert Hunter, Chamberlain of the Lordship of Zetland.

Early travellers were most concerned with the exposed location of the manse at Neap, amongst them Samuel Hibbert in 1822: *'On the summit of the Noup of Nesting, the manse of the respectable minister of the parish is situated. It was built by one of his predecessors, on a site better adapted for a lighthouse.'*

Finnie

Lunna Kirk with its notable tree and Lunna House

Excellent armorial panel commemorating the marriage of Thomas Hunter and Grisella Bruce in 1707. Curious pilasters on two corners are part joined to the building. A decorative plaster ceiling and some refined woodwork inside. *A seasonal hotel*. Although remote, the Hunters kept up with southern fashions; on axis with the house, beyond the former, grass-grown, approach, are spiky gate pillars. Behind these, atop a rocky mound, foundations of an early religious site remain. Further up the hill, a now ruinous building in Gothick style and straddling a dyke on the summit, closing the vista, is a rough stone-arched *folly*. Here the Hunters are said to have watched the comings and goings of their tenants should they be trading with other merchants. Lunna has its own excellent stone harbour beside which is a well-preserved 19th-century lime-burning kiln of beehive shape, looking like a tiny broch.

Lunna's seclusion and its position on the east coast nearer to Norway attracted David Howarth He set up Lunna as the first base of the 'Shetland Bus', shuttling over to Norway during the Second World War supplying the underground there and returning with refugees, using Norwegian fishing boats and crew.

St Margaret, Lunna Kirk, 1753
Built by the fourth Hunter of Lunna on the site of a family mausoleum (and possibly earlier chapel) the kirk is a small rectangle with a rear forestair to the gallery. Massive buttresses on the side, one of which has what is said to be a

leper's squint which allowed the afflicted to hear
the service without coming into contact with the
congregation. The interior is a gem; compact
gallery on three sides around the pulpit. Beside
this an 18th-century memorial and in the porch
two Hunter stones from the 1600s. In the
kirkyard a notable tree huddles for shelter
between the buttresses. Simple memorials to
lost Norwegians. Nearby a roofless **fishing
booth**, storage below, and outside steps to upper
accommodation. The fish-drying beach is partly
manmade. Between the kirk and the booth only
greener grass gives away the swathe made by
the landfall of the Ninian pipeline *en route* to
Sullom Voe.

Fishing booth on the beach, Lunna

NORTH   MAINLAND
North Mainland occupies a large land area
divided into two distinctive areas. The
southernmost part, stretching from Voe to
Mossbank, includes those areas of Shetland
most affected by the oil boom in the 1970s and
early 1980s. The northern part is the nearly
detached parish of Northmavine, with some of
Shetland's finest coastal scenery.

Voe

43 **Voe**
A fiordside settlement, clustering around a

House, Lower Voe

fishing station developed by the Adies in the mid-19th century, and used latterly for weaving and knitting. This most Scandinavian of locations is now in decline. Further out Olna Firth, the Norwegian Whaling Co operated a whaling station from 1904 until the decline of Shetland whaling in 1928. **Voe House** is a plain, late 18th-century, house of two storeys and five bays, built for the tenant of the Voe sheepwalk by the Giffords of Busta. **House**, Lower Voe, 1986, Peter Johnson
The architect's own tall, white house.

Old Olnafirth Kirk, *c*.1700
An empty shell with arched doorways. At the north end the aisle of the Giffords of Busta was reached by a forestair. The ruinous chamber below has an armorial panel to Thomas Gifford and Elizabeth Mitchell, married in 1714 (when he also extended Busta House thereby providing for death as well as married life), above the arched entrance. Two Gifford memorials inside. Above Voe, on Susetter Hill, is a large commercial **aerogenerator**, 1988-9.

Below *North Mainland Swimming Pool*. Bottom *Voxter*. Right *Brae, post oil*

44 **Brae**
All the features of a Western frontier town: massive and hurried expansion in the 1970s attempted to meet the needs of a flood of personnel for Sullom Voe, and resulted in featureless housing estates. Old Brae remains, a little church, a good manse and **Brae House**, a substantial merchant's house with its own pier. Brae **Junior Secondary School**, 1981, Baxter Clark & Paul, updates this practice's earlier schools in Shetland with gentle pitched roofs and projecting window bays. The **North Mainland Swimming Pool**, 1988, Faulkner Browns, complete with palm, is cloaked with a bright blue metal roof with glazed apex lighting.

Voxter House, 1869, a manse of some quality, was converted to an Outdoor Centre in 1985 by

Richard Gibson. At nearby **Trondavoe**, a
crofthouse below the road retains a wooden lum
projecting through the felt ridge, detached from
the gable.

BP Development Ltd

45 **Sullom Voe Oil Terminal**, from 1973
Completed in 1982, Sullom Voe consists of a
paraphenalia of tanks and equipment
comprising Europe's largest oil terminal. There
is surprisingly little visual impact, since the
expanse of land, sea and sky overpowers even
the largest oil tanker. It is more visible at night
when flare stacks light the sky. Its size is more
indicated by facts: up to 6000 men were involved
in the construction, and Orka Voe was filled
with peat from the site. Award-winning
landscape by W J Cairns & Partners. The
terminal is served by a revived wartime
aerodrome at Scatsta.

These lands were the Garth Estate, the Old
House of Garth long vanished. Nineteenth-
century **Garth House**, alongside the access road
to the oil terminal, was the farmhouse. Below
flare stacks is a so-called **Pony Pund**, a large
square, stone, fortress filled with lean-to
shelters formerly used to breed blackface sheep
(and/or ponies). Taller corners prevented
livestock climbing out. **Firth** is all housing
schemes. Note the white-painted haa, much
altered, at **Mossbank**. Another **Pony Pund** at

Sullom Voe Terminal

The father of architect James
Playfair, and grandfather of William
Henry Playfair, was chaplain at
Busta before he became minister at
Liff and Benvie in Tayside.

At **Mavis Grind**, the Atlantic and
North Sea come within yards of each
other but the romance of the spot
has been destroyed by massive
quarrying. Note the Second World
War tank traps.

*The Pony Pund at Swinister with
multiple ayres behind*

Finnie

The **Giffords of Busta** were descended from a Scots minister who came to Northmavine and developed a taste for land. Thomas Gifford became laird in the early 1700s, built up a fortune as a merchant and fish exporter and held the positions of Steward Depute of Shetland and Chamberlain to the Earldom. His estates were the islands' largest. In 1748 his four sons were drowned in the voe leaving him without an heir until a maid announced that she had been secretly married to the eldest son and was bearing his child. The resulting grandson, Gideon, was brought up at Busta: the mother, Barbara Pitcairn, lived out her life as a poor relation in Lerwick. Gideon became laird but died leaving no direct heir. Resultant lengthy lawsuits left the estate impoverished.

Right *Busta House*. Below *Olwell Knowe, Busta*. Bottom *Busta House, the entrance*. Bottom right *Hillswick House*

Swinster is spectacularly sited near multiple ayres joining an island to mainland. The Haa of Swinister sits on the northernmost.

46 **Busta House**, now hotel, said to date from 1588 A tall, white, Scots house, the earliest part two storeys with crowsteps. In 1714, Thomas Gifford married Elizabeth Mitchell (of Westshore, Scalloway) and added a three-storey mansion. Their armorial panel is above the arched entrance. Dressed window surrounds and spiral skewputts. A massive and harmonious addition, designed by Peter Watts, was added in 1984. Little remains of the original interior. Leafy grounds with scattered gargoyles acquired from a past restoration of the House of Commons. Beyond the splendid stone harbour is a little rubbly drum doocot, probably contemporary with Gifford additions. Rough nesting boxes in the thickness of the walls.

Olwell Knowe, 1986, Alan McDonald Radiating forms in concrete and glass, partly grass covered, grow out from a knoll. **Muckle Roe** is a large, round, red granite isle, connected by road bridge to Mainland since the 1950s. Some crofthouses retain their thatch.

47 **Hillswick** was the terminus of the West Side steamer and being close to splendid scenery

became a destination for tourists. It was possible to sail to here from Leith. **St Magnus Bay Hotel**, *c.*1900, was erected for cruise passengers, by the North of Scotland, Orkney & Shetland Steam Navigation Co Ltd. A timber structure imported from Norway. Two storeys of timber cladding with steep roofs and decorative gable trusses in 'Swiss' style. The hall and dining room, lined in pine, retain some period atmosphere.

Hillswick House, late 18th century on earlier foundations
A symmetrical group, the main house has a Venetian doorway. The right flanking wing forms the **Booth** public house which, it is said, has given service since Adolf Westerman, a Hamburg Merchant, had a booth here in 1684. Notice the shell-clad shed along the beach.

Northmavine Kirk, 1733, is a huge barn with two tiers of pointed windows. The galleried interior was rebuilt *c.*1825 to hold 600.
Northmavine Manse, 1768, a decent two-storey, T-plan harled house with a steep roof, looks like a contemporary Scots laird's house. The cemetery on low ground is round, encircled by a wall.

Haa of Tangwick, 18th century,
The Haa of Cheyne of Tangwick, with thick harled walls, deep-set windows and a slated roof. Restored 1987 by Peter Johnson Partnership, the clean white interior with a pine stair serves as a local museum: *open in summer.*

Stenness has a rocky beach circled by the

Left *St Magnus Bay Hotel.* Above *Tangwick Haa*

At **Hamnavoe** is the decaying cottage of Johnny 'Notion' Williamson, a local pioneer in the use of vaccines against smallpox. *'Unassisted by education, and unfettered by the rules of art ... He is careful in providing the best matter and keeps it a long time before he puts it to use — sometimes 7 or 8 years. And, in order to lessen its virulence, he first dries it in peat smoke, and then puts it under ground covered in camphor ... by a small knife, made by his own hands, he gently raises a very little of the outer skin of the arm ... then puts in a very small quantity of the matter ... The only plaister he uses, for healing the wound, is a bit of cabbage leaf.'*

'The Landlords to render them [their tenants] more dependent, never granting them Leases, the wretched Inhabitants holding their small Farms from year to year. The Tennants are bound to fish for their Landlords, giving all they catch above a certain Size at a stated Price. They are held in a State little better than Slavery.'
J Ker, 1780

remains of fishing booths and lodges, used during the summer haaf-fishing by men fishing for their landlords. They fished from sixerns (six-oared, six-man, open boats) and old men and boys washed, salted and dried the catch on the stony beach. The lodges were occupied from May and often partly dismantled at the end of the season.

Eshaness Kirkyard, is the site of the old **Cross Kirk**, which was a place of pilgrimage until 1664 when a zealous minister, Hercules Sinclair, had it cast down. An elaborate monument to the Cheynes of Tangwick is attached to a remnant of the old fabric.

Above *Memorial in Eshaness Kirkyard*. Right *Eshaness Lighthouse*

In **Eshaness Kirkyard**: *'Donald Robertson, born 14th January 1785, died 4th June 1848, aged 63 years. He was a peaceable, quiet man and to all appearance a sincere Christian. His death was much regretted which was caused by the stupidity of Laurence Tulloch of Clothister (Sullom) who sold him nitre instead of Epsom salts by which he was killed in the space of 5 hours after taking a dose of it.'*

48 **Eshaness Lighthouse**, 1929, David A and Charles Stevenson
A short, square, sparkling tower above flat-roofed accommodation, economy dictating the square plan as interior fittings were not required to fit curved walls. Visible on a promontory into the Loch of Houlland is the unexcavated rubble mound of a broch. The mass of rock gives some indication of the material and labour involved in its erection. *'Here the ruins of the Burgh of Howland, built into a loch, fortified towards the land with a very thick rampart of vast stones.'*

49 **Ollaberry**
Formerly a fishing station. A good 19th-century stone pier remains. Fishing booths at the pier head have been converted into houses. In the **Kirkyard**, attached to a fragment of an old church, is an elaborate memorial: a shattered panel with family arms framed by Corinthian-capped columns and a pediment; erected in

The Stenness fishing station

Fethaland
'The whole was like a great ship, for there were none present but weatherbeaten seamen, not a woman was to be seen in the hamlet. The inside of these huts corresponds with the outside. You will find nothing but some beds made of rude boards, nailed together, containing straw and course blankets...'
Christian Ployen, the Danish Government's representative in Faroe, commenting on Fethaland in 1839.

1754, the mason was John Forres. The present church is *c.*1865. **Ollaberry Haa**, 1789, is a stern, Georgian, rendered haa with an ashlar porch, restored in 1972 by Richard Moira. It was built for Andrew Gifford, whose son Arthur sought to have himself made heir-in-line to Thomas Gifford of Busta who had died in 1760. Another haa at nearby **Bardister**. **Lochend House** is the extended 18th-century haa of the Nicolsons of Lochend. **North Roe**, the northernmost part of Mainland, has an 1870 Church of Scotland. North Haa sits beyond the 50 beach. **Fethaland** was a haaf-fishing station convenient for the fishing grounds up to 35 miles offshore. The shells of lodges remain. The minor light is one of several built to guide oil tankers into Sullom Voe.

Left A contemporary view of the Fethaland fishing station. Below *The classical monument in Ollaberry Kirkyard*

The **White Wife** (*above*) stares from
the Otterswick shore at Queyon. She
is a figurehead from the training
ship *Bohus* outward bound from
Gothenburg when it went aground
here, in 1924, with the loss of four
lives. She was restored in 1989.

Right *St Colman's Episcopal
Church*. Below *The Old Haa of
Brough, Burravoe*

YELL

The largest of the Northern isles. The main road
rushes through the largely peat-covered interior:
'*so uncouth a place that no creature can live
therein unless he be born there.*' Side roads
reveal a much greater diversity of scenery.

51 Arrival, by ferry, is at **Ulsta**. **Pier House**, the
shop, is a straightforward 19th-century cottage.
A wooden forestair serving the upper floor is
supported on massive stone corbels.

St Magnus (South Yell) Kirk,
Hamnavoe, *c.*1838
A tall rendered box with a little openwork belfry.
Shallow arched windows, three levels of which
light the gable. The interior is later, the gallery
now blocked off. A board lists the ministers of
the parish dating back to the 16th century.

52 **Burravoe**, South Yell's main settlement, is
clustered untidily above the shoreline amidst
remains of former fishing and trading activity.
There is a broch mound, topped by a ruined
skeo; a drystone building for drying fish and
meat in the wind.

St Colman's Espiscopal Church, 1900,
R T N Spier
A little rural gem, lacking a woodland setting, in
Arts & Crafts Gothic with an apsidal end and
spirelet. All is of the finest quality: dressed stone
and rubble exterior matched by the interior with
open roof. The amateur architect owned the
estate of Culdees in Perthshire and designed a
number of Episcopal churches.

Old Haa of Brough, 1672,
The Tyries, merchants, built their haa where
they could over-see the entrance into Burravoe,
and operated a trading booth down by the shore.

Finnie

The road had always passed through the haa's courtyard, but its widening caused the demolition of the opposite range of buildings. Two arches remain, the southern with a weathered panel over. Harled, buttressed, walls with crowstep gables and deepset windows. Restored in 1987 as a local visitors' centre: open in summer.

Along the beach lies the faded mid 19th century **Manor House**. A curious seaside villa, it was formed from two connected houses and fronted by a verandah and gazebo added in the 1920s.

Northwards from Burravoe, ruinous **Grossabrough** and **Swarister Haas** stare at each other across a splendid beach. **Otterswick Methodist Chapel** is a simple rural kirk. The corrugated-iron old **East Yell Hall** has more strength of character than its bland replacement.

Barbara Garriock

Top *Old Haa of Brough.* Above *A contemporary photograph of the Old Haa of Brough when the road passed through its courtyard*

53 **Mid Yell**

The island's main community. **St John's (Mid Yell) Kirk**, 1832, is a little T-plan kirk. The old shoreline **Kirkyard** contains relics of the earlier kirk — an arched doorway peeps above the turf. Splendid memorial dated 1730 with armorial panel and columns and, in an enclosure, tombstones of the lairds of Windhouse dating from *c.*1690. In decay at the pierhead, is

Above Haa of Gardie. Right Mid Yell Kirkyard with the remains of the earlier St Johns

Linkshouse, 1770, a plain merchant's house of two floors. **Lussetter House**, 18th century, is a T-plan, two-storeyed former manse, later outworks in toy fort castellated style.

Yell Leisure Centre, 1988, Faulkner Browns A slick package of leisure pool and sports hall (with tropical foliage) within a low profile, metal-roofed shell. An example of Oil revenue benefitting the further flung communities. The empty **Haa of Gardie**, sturdy with a rusty-red iron roof, was once the home of Laurence Williamson, a Shetland historian. **Gardiesting**, possibly from 1645, is a dour and substantial early haa. Note the tiny house uphill, clad in opened out, flattened oil drums.

Right Pony Pund, Kirkabister. Below Burraness Broch

Kirkabister has another of Shetland's four 'pony studs': a smallish, complete and isolated enceinte in a wide landscape. Of **Burraness Broch**, a remote and strategic location commanding the seas between Yell, Unst and Fetlar, the east face stands festooned in lichen, to over 4m (13 ft).

St Olaf's (North Yell) Kirk, *c.*1830, is the usual rectangular kirk but sporting a peculiar crenellated frontage, newly covered in spotty dry dash. Around Culli Voe some ancient-looking booths. **Greenbank House** is 19th-century.

54

Kirk of Ness (St Olaf's), Breakon, medieval
Still a considerable structure in the 19th
century, blown sand has now almost overcome
this pre-Reformation kirk, abandoned in 1750.
At **Houlland**, the haa of *c.*1735 lost its roof a
century ago to a low felted replacement as the
house was *'splitting in twa.'* Pretty range of
outbuildings and the *Minerva*: a retired fourern
now providing superior accommodation for hens.
The haa at **Midbrake** again *c.*1735, is now a
store with a bold rubbly porch. The elegant 18th
55 century **Gloup Haa** has been restored. Beyond,
the sentimental and lumpy **Memorial** to an
1881 fishing diaster: 58 men from ten sixerns,
six of these from the Gloup Haaf Station, were
lost when overcome by a July storm.

Top *St Olaf's (North Yell) Kirk.*
Above *Kirk of Ness drawn by Henry
Dryden, 1855.* Left top *Houses at
Cullivoe.* Left middle *Haa of
Houlland and 'the Minerva'.* Left
bottom *The Gloup fishermen's
memorial and Haa, behind*

North Haa's fine classical frontage

'. . . At West Sandwick I found,
beside a really beautiful mansion, a
regular farm-yard with excellent
stables and out-houses, large
enclosures both under cultivation
and as pasture, the commencement of
roads, ploughs, harrows, rollers,
sowing machines, and artificial
foddering of cattle in full operation.'
Christian Ployen, 1839

Windhouse

56 **North Haa**, West Sandwick, 18th century, is a
mansion of two interconnected parallel blocks.
That to the rear was added c.1820 as was the
showy facade. The main block is two storeys and
the usual prominent garret. The principal floor
has a central, round-headed window flanked by
tri-partite windows. Porch is pedimented, as are
the side office wings with their Venetian
windows.

Windhouse, from 1707, said to be haunted,
ruinous, glowers down on to the road in one of
Yell's gloomier parts. Reconstructed c.1880 to
become a one-and-a-half storey villa with side
wings, crowsteps and more castellations.
Armorial panel. Possibly the only Shetland
property to possess a lodge (now ruined).

UNST
Shetland's northernmost isle, as a contrast after
Yell, consists of gentle green slopes and bare,
rock strewn hills of serpentine.

Belmont, c.1777
A miniature, dressy, mansion joined by
quadrant walls to little pyramid roofed
pavilions. The doorway has a finely carved
cornice (protected until recent years by a porch).
A central Venetian window above and a niche
within a thin pediment. Quality interior with a
curved staircase. All awaits restoration.
Grounds sweep to the sea. Contemporary farm
steading behind the house. Belmont was built
for Thomas Mouat, son of Mouat of Garth, and
before building, he had toured Lothian to
acquaint himself with the latest fashions.

Finnie

Top *Belmont.* Middle *Uyeasound with the impressive standing stone.* Bottom *Uyeasound Kirk*

Finnie

Finnie

57 The village of **Uyeasound** straggles the coastline. **Greenwell's Booth** is the empty rubble shell of a trading booth erected by local merchants, the Scotts. Small, thick walled houses along the shore westwards. Gabled, seaside **Maundeville**, dated 1882, in painted brickwork would be much more at home on an English coast. The **Church of Scotland**, (former UF) 1843, is a wide, shallow gabled, Disruption kirk with belfry and round headed doorway; it looks almost rustic Italianate.

Right *Muness Castle in 1792.* Centre *Muness Castle.* Bottom *Muness Castle, Shothole*

National Library of Scotland

Finnie

Finnie

Muness Castle, 1598

Encouraged by his half-brother Robert Stewart, Laurence Bruce of Cultmalindie (Perthshire) fled to Shetland after involvement in some murderous affray, and established a rule as tyrannous as Stewart's. Muness, designed probably by Andrew Crawford (who was to build Scalloway Castle) since similar features appear in both, is Z-plan: an oblong main block with round towers diagonally opposite. Angle turrets, whose distinctive corbelling remain, occupy the other corners. Note the incredible variety of decorative shotholes throughout the structure. The entrance door surround was brought here in recent times from Lund. Two carved panels above, one commemorating the castle's erection by Laurence Bruce — *'that worthy man'*. From the vaulted ground floor of kitchen and stores, a scale-and-platt stair leads to the main hall and formerly continued to the floor above. The laird's private accommodation occupied two floors in a palace block at the far end, inter-connected by a private staircase. Windy now, but there was considerable comfort and convenience, and the plan form was comparable to a contemporary

French chateau. **Sandwick Beach** is the site of Norse settlements (part lost to erosion) probably from the 12th century onwards.

Boardastubble, Shetland's largest standing stone marks the way to the **Old House of Lund**, 18th century, a derelict mansion built for John Ross, a merchant. Its original doorway (from behind the later Georgian porch) is now at Muness.

St Olaf's Chapel, Lund, *c.*1200
Remaining in use until 1785, this rubble rectangle still rises to the wallheads, with an arched entrance in the west gable. On the underside of the internal window lintel is a faintly incised Christian fish symbol. Inside, memorials to the Unst branch of the Mouats of Garth and the 1573 slab of *Segebad Detkin*, merchant and burgher of Bremen. Another outside to *Henrik Segeleken The Elder*, also of Bremen, who died in 1585. Ancient little rude stone crosses in the kirkyard. Opposite Lund, on the slope at **Underhoull**, are the excavated remains of a Norse house. There are doubtless many more throughout Shetland, concealed on sites continuously occupied since. **Westing Watermill** is a little horizontal watermill still in full working order.

Top *Mealhouse, Westings Clack Mill.* Above *St John's, Baltasound.* Left *Lund Kirk, the old house of Lund on the right skyline*

58 **Baltasound** is the loosely scattered main settlement of Unst. Little remains of the years around 1905, when Baltasound was prominent in the herring fishery, with as many as 600 boats crowding the sound, and over 2000 gutters and coopers housed in timber huts.

St John's, *c.*1827 and 1959
The original vast Georgian box, said to have

Sports Centre, Unst

seated 2000, was demolished and rebuilt on part
of the earlier foundations, and the remainder
can still be seen along with urns scattered from
the wallhead. The present church has an
openwork belfry and an airy interior with tall,
round-headed, windows. At Baliasta is the
roofless shell of the **Old Kirk**, 1764, in its
kirkyard. Nearby **Hillside Church**, Shetland's
first Free Church, 1843, is identical to that at
Uyeasound but roofless. **Unst Sports Centre**,
1988, Faulkner Browns, is identical to that at
Mid Yell.

Buness

The **Buness lairds** are unique in
that they claim to be able to trace
their lineage back to Norse times.
Henrik Hendrickson (changing to
Henderson) was foud (chief law
officer) of Shetland in 1450. Buness
passed by family descent to the
Sandersons and latterly the
Edmondstons.

Buness, possibly from 17th century
A plain, rendered, two-storey haa of six bays,
(the western three added later) and crowstepped
gables. A 19th-century wing was blown up in
1955. An upright slab in the grounds
commemorates research into gravitational
acceleration at a high latitude by Frenchman
Jean-Baptiste Biot in 1817. Buness has a
delicate timber porch (one of many elegant
porches throughout Unst, often in various

Gothic and classical styles).

Hagdale Horsemill, *c.*1917, at the now redundant chromate quarry at Hagdale, was used to process low-grade ore. By 1921 higher-grade imported ores had forced its closure. The circular, roofless, mill retains its grinding stones and the water channel which washed the grindings.

Haroldswick has some older houses along the sea, one with flanking booths. Britain's northernmost **Post Office** has a red-painted (and much-photographed) timber frontage. **RAF Saxa Vord** is Unst's main employer. Assorted, nondescript, buildings from the 1950s onwards are fortunately concentrated in one enclave and are being redeveloped. All has been improved by **Accommodation**, from 1982, Property Services Agency. Much research has produced steep-pitched roofs, gabled ends and robust detailing. Fine hard landscaping.

At **Norwick**, the kirkyard, an early site, has small, rough, stone crosses. *'So far I live to the Northward, No man lives North of me...'* The northernmost house, **Skaw**, is neat and white. An upturned boat roofs a shed.

Muckle Flugga Light, 1858, David & Thomas Stevenson
This rock light is a short tower with lantern,

Top *Buness drawn by the Rev James Everett in 1828.* Left *Accommodation and Officers Mess, Saxa Vord.* Middle *Horse Mill, Hagdale.* Above *Muckle Flugga Light*

now encumbered by later additions. Built of
brick for ease of transport, the light was
constructed after bitter argument between the
Commissioners of Northern Lighthouses and the
Board of Trade (Trinity House). On David
Stevenson's advice, the Commissioners had
advised against such a wild site, but worried
that war in the Crimea might spread to
northern seas, Trinity House insisted that the
Commissioners' *'eminent engineer'* would
overcome any difficulties. The shore station at
Burrafirth has the usual flat-roofed keeper's
house.

Shetland Museum

Finnie

Top *Brough Lodge, c. 1930.* Above
Fetlar Manse

FETLAR
'The garden of Shetland' lies south of Unst and
east of Yell. Fetlar has many ancient sites, and
Funziegert, a neolothic boundary dyke crosses
much of the north of the island.

Brough Lodge, *c.*1820
A grotesque mass in decay, the main part
chunky Gothic (the original flat roof has been
altered), the entrance to the court debased
classical. There are various 'Gothick'
excrescences in stone and brick, the whole
horribly kitsch. **Folly**, behind on the hilltop, is
in the form of a crenellated round tower. Brough
Lodge was built for Arthur Nicolson of Lochend
who had bought most of Fetlar from the Bruces.
By claiming the inheritance of a distant relation,
he became Sir Arthur Nicolson in 1826, and
under the Nicolsons, much of Fetlar was cleared.

Fetlar Kirk, 1790, is a simple country kirk,
narrow, thus appearing taller. Round-headed
windows and belfry. Old memorials in the
kirkyard, one built into the kirk wall, another
with pilasters and pediment. The 1756 **Fetlar
Manse** is a harled T-plan house, window
surrounds picked out in black and sheltering

behind trees. It contrasts with the normal severe Haa form of country houses as John Tudor, a traveller, *c.*1880, noted: *'The manse of Tresta is, with the exception of that of Tingwall, the most beautifully situated parsonage in the islands, and covered as it is in summertime with wild trailing honey-suckle, and surrounded by small elderberry trees, has a very south of Pentland Firth look about it.'*

Leagarth House, with the Ripple Stone in front

Leagarth House, Hubie, 1900

A large plain gabled villa: a showpiece in its heyday boasting a walled garden, exotic plants and a private electricity supply. Extensive glazed outbuildings and a hall which was formerly used by the community. This was the home of Sir William Watson Cheyne, assistant to Lord Lister. Aitken of Lerwick was the contractor and may have been architect. In front of the house is a standing monolith, the Ripple Stone.

Aithsbank, 18th century

A solid two-storey house, sadly decaying, grey harl, thick walls and tiny windows. The beach below the kailyard was a fish-curing station, *c.*1840.

Round House

The rubble remains of a summerhouse built by Arthur Nicolson on cleared land, the timber structure on top is long vanished. Scattered columns remain. Nicolson is said to have only spent one night here owing to 'noises'. **Funzie** was another fish-curing beach; it retains traces of booths and workings. **Urie**, in the north of the island, was another. **Smithfield**, 1816, is a once elegant merchants haa.

The **Hanseatic League** was a trading body of merchants and shipowners centred on Lubeck and operating from Russia to Portugal, its influence peaking in the 14th century. In Shetland, Hansa trade lasted 500 years, first by the way of the League's 'Kontor' in Bergen, then as illicit trade became the norm, direct with Hamburg and Bremen. Stockfish (dried and salted cod and ling) was exported, luxury goods imported. The Germans retained their trade by extending credit from one season to the next. A decline in activities at the end of the 17th century came about by the emergence of Scottish merchants and then local merchant-lairds, famine, disease and war when the French plundered German ships. The final demise was the 1707 Act of Union which favoured local commercial activity.

Finnie

Symbister

WHALSAY
A prosperous island lying off East Mainland; dependent on its large fishing fleet.

Symbister, the main settlement is tiered up from its **Harbour**. Continuous activity from the 17th century is represented by old stone dock and stores, one tall with a high, blocked up entrance. Along the beach is a **Skeo**, stone built with wall slits to ventilate fish which were once dried on the stony beach.

Symbister, Pier House

Shetland Museum

Pier House, supposedly 17th century or earlier A Hanseatic trading booth projecting its prow end seawards by a fine stone harbour. Two diminutive storeys with a hoist for lifting goods from ships. Alteration, *c.*1830, is indicated by cut granite blocks in the gables. Fine restoration in 1984 by Richard Gibson, using traditional methods of construction. At the pierhead is **Bremen Booth**. The basement of this harbourside house may be the booth occupied by Herman Schroder when it was attacked and destroyed by pirates in 1563. The road uphill was formerly known as Bremer Strasse.

Symbister House (now school), 1823 Frosty classical, in hard grey granite from Nesting (East Mainland). This, Shetland's most outstanding Georgian building, was built *'at the enormous expense... of £30,000'* by the sixth Robert Bruce of Symbister. It dominates

Shetland Museum

Symbister as the Bruces did their tenants. Three
bays, the centre advanced with a portico of
coupled cast iron columns approached by a stair.
The house has been disfigured following
conversion in the 1940s to the island's school.
Behind, extensive ranges of symmetrical offices,
stables and coachhouses, altered and decaying.
A delicate belfry and tall castellated doocot
tower (the toilet was below). Scattered urns. The
best, and possibly largest, of Shetland's armorial
panels, moved here from elsewhere, dated 1750
and inscribed John Bruce Steuart and Christina
Gifford, sculpted by John Forbes. The **Old Haa**,
18th century or earlier, is the much-altered
former residence of the Bruces. The garden wall
remains with arched gateways.

Finnie

Top *Symbister House before
conversion.* Above *Whalsay Kirk*

Sports Centre, 1990, Faulkner Browns
Another leisure complex similar to Yell and
Unst. **Whalsay Kirk**, 18th century, is dour and
plain, with a little belfry, the northern wing a
vaulted chamber below and a vestry above,
reached by forestair. It occupies an earlier
church site on Kirk Ness.

Standing Stones of Yoxie and Benie House,
3rd-2nd millenium *BC*
Two large excavated houses, walls remain up to
1.2m (4ft) high. These were probably important
settlements. **Loch of Huxter Fort** is an Iron
Age structure, linked to the shore by a
causeway. Much rubble including a blockhouse
with side cells.

Hugh MacDiarmid (C M Grieve),
with his wife and son, *'survived
virtually penniless'* from 1933 to
1942 in a cottage at **Sodom** (from
Sudheim — the southern part of the
original settlement). In *The
Uncanny Scot*, MacDiarmid relates a
three-day sojourn on uninhabited
West Linga, surviving with only
matches, tobacco, books and
catching fish with a bent pin and
string. Poetic licence expanded on a
day visit he made with the crofter of
the island.

OUT SKERRIES

Finnie

Crofthouses, Skerries

East, beyond Whalsay are rocky islands, of less than one square mile, enclosing a natural harbour. **Housay** and **Bruray**, the main islands, were connected by road bridge in 1957 replacing a much earlier footbridge. **Bound Skerry Light**, 1858, by David & Thomas Stevenson, is a white, stone built tapering rock tower rising to 30m (98 ft). It cost £21,000: 90% above Stevenson's estimate. Keepers' houses and stores are on neighbouring **Grunay**.

BRESSAY

The Dutch recognised the importance of Bressay, protecting as it does the eastern side of Bressay Sound. Along with fledgeling Lerwick, Bressay contributed to trade with the Dutch fishing fleets to the distress of the authorities in Scalloway. An Act of 1615 forbade anyone to go to the island of Bressay *'for furnishing of beir, vivoris and uther necessaris to the Hollandaris and utheris foirren (eris) committing thairby villanie, fornicatioun and adultrie'*. An old saying was *'Amsterdam was biggit oot o' da back o' Bressay'*. Bressay shares with Mousa supplies of good flat bedded building stone and stone slates were formerly quarried and supplied to the rest of Shetland.

Notable Out Skerries shipwrecks include Dutch East-Indiamen, the *Kennemerland* in 1664, and *De Liefde*, in 1711. They were sailing *'Achter Om'* — the long way around Britain to avoid enemy in the English channel, *en route* to Java. *Below* Skerries Lighthouse.

Finnie

Maryfield House, mid 19th century
Typical late haa (now hotel) but retaining tall proportions with a dominant garret. The house has its own landing stage and store house. Constructed by the Garth estate factor, Walker, a Scot brought in to improve the land, the house was named after his wife. Walker *'made da uproar'* by clearing tenants off the land here and elsewhere in Shetland in the 1860s and early 1870s to make way for sheep.

Above *Gardie House, c.1812 drawn by A M Skene. Note the farm steading on the hill behind.* Left *Gardie House*

Gardie House, from 1724

One of Shetland's principal lairds' houses, built for the Hendersons before passing to the Mouats of Garth. Constructed as a double-width plan, an innovation for Shetland imported along with Forbes, the mason, from Aberdeen. The show front is to the sea. Seven-bay, two-storey with garret, brown-harled, a little relief is gained from stone surrounds and quoins. Largely unaltered save for the square ashlar porch of 1810 and the enlargement of upper-floor accommodation forming a central pediment by John M Aitken of Lerwick *c.*1905, tempering what were probably more ambitious proposals by John Bryce of Edinburgh. The rear and side elevations are much less regular. The principal apartments are on the first floor, the drawing room with fine timber panelling to the same pattern as at the Haa of Sand (West Mainland). A relocated armorial panel from Garth in Delting has had its date recut unconvincingly as 1579. A good stone-built harbour beyond the main gate of rusticated urn capped pilasters

Walter Scott was entertained at Gardie in 1814: '*... we are most hospitably treated at Gardie. Young Mr Mowat, son of my old friend, is an improver, and a moderate one. He has got a ploughman from Scotland who acts as a grieve, but as yet with the prejudices and inconveniences which usually attach themselves to the most salutary experiments.*'

83

Garden gates at Gardie

Finnie

with attached columns. A diminutive **stable block** is topped by a square pyramid roof with weathervane. A picturesque **cottage**, early 19th century, extended later in mass concrete, has Gothic windows, that in the porch original with timber tracery. On the hill behind Gardie, the symmetrical steading of farmhouse flanked by blind arcaded gables, much altered, testifies to the land improvements.

The main community straggles the shoreline southwards, the road deviating around the **Kirk**, 1815. A typical ha'rled box with belfry replacing its *c.*1722 predecessor which in turn replaced Bressay's three ancient chapels. Stained glass, one window commemorating Sir Robert Cruickshank, son of the manse, who became Governor of Tasmania in 1886. **Mizpah House**, 1819. Constructed as the manse in usual sober haa form. Kirkabister was the site of St John's, one of the early chapels.

Bressay Lighthouse

Finnie

Bressay Lighthouse, 1858,
David & Thomas Stevenson
A stubby tower with corbelled parapet, accompanied by two blocks of keepers' accommodation, the whole group encircled by a perimeter wall, all sparkling white. The promontory of the **Bard** has a 6-in. gun from the First World War. Similar guns remain at Aiths Voe in the north of the island.

Gunnista Kirkyard. Site of the medieval kirk of St Olaf, contains the rectangular hollow 18th-century mausoleum to the Hendersons of

Finnie

Ancient grave slabs within the walls of the former St Mary's, Cullingsburgh

Gardie. Rubble with a classical ashlar facing and cornice, now much decayed. Note the skull carved on the keystone. Some old graveslabs.

St Mary's, Cullingsburgh
Splendid coastal location approached on foot across a beach and past a ruinous crofting township. In use until the early 18th century, low walls remain of the late medieval cross-plan church on the site of a Celtic predecessor all within the confines of a broch mound. Within the church, memorials from the 17th century include a table slab and tombstone, dated 27 August 1636, inscribed in Dutch to *Claes Jansen Bruyn* of Durgendam, captain of a Dutch East Indiaman. From this site came the *c.*10th-century Bressay stone, decorated with beasts and knotwork and inscribed with ogham writings (now in the National Museum of Antiquities, Edinburgh). Above, crowning **Ander Hill**, is a coastguard watchtower from the First World War, in rubble with concrete dressings.

NOSS
Reached by a short ferry trip across the turbulent sound (seasonal). On the Bressay side, below abandoned crofts, is the prominant mound of a ruined **broch**. Subject to clearances Noss was depopulated by 1939. The farmhouse of **Gungstie**, possibly from 17th century and restored in 1986, is rubble built, one-and-a-half storey with few windows and three massive chimneys. Slabs remain from a chapel site last used for the burial of victims of a shipwreck in 1870.

Noss Pony Pund, *c.*1870; restored 1986
The usual regular enclosure complete with slated lean-to stock shelters. Noss was leased by Garth Estate to the Marquis of Londonderry from 1870 and used for the breeding of Shetland ponies for his Durham coal mines. The aim was

Noss from Bressay. Note the broch mound on the Bressay shore

Finnie

Cradle of Noss

'...two ropes are stretched across the chasm, and strongly secured to a post placed on the rock for that purpose: a sort of square box is procured, 3ft long and 2ft broad, termed a cradle, having an upright piece of wood about 4in. square at each of its corners, projecting a few inches beyond the box, with holes sufficiently large to admit the ends of the ropes, which are passed through them, and fastened very firmly to the island. The bottom of this cradle is made by course rope lacing, to render the seat easy for any person passing over ...' Thus described by Richard Drosier, 1828. In 1814 Walter Scott made a visit and recorded: *'This detached rock is wholly inaccessible, unless by a pass of peril, entitled the **Cradle of Noss**, which is a sort of wooden chair, travelling from precipice to precipice on rings, which run upon two cables stretched across the gulf. We viewed this extraordinary contrivance from beneath, at the distance of perhaps one hundred fathoms at least. The boatmen made light of the risk of crossing it, but it must be tremendous to be a brain disposed to be giddy. Seen from beneath, a man in the basket would resemble a large crow or raven floating between rock and rock. The purpose of this strange contrivance is to give the tenant the benefit of putting a few sheep upon the Holm, the top of which is level and affords good pasture.'* In 1842, Wilson got a bit carried away: *'We felt as if we had been endowed with some newly acquired and supernatural power, which enabled us thus to float in air as freely and as fearlessly as a strong-winged bird of prey, and thus supposing ourself an eagle, we doubt not had we clutched a gull we should have eaten it upon the spot. Indeed our chief reason for not remaining longer so suspended was a peculiar feathery feeling all over, with a strange sensation more especially about the nose and feet, as if the former was becoming hard, horny, aquiline, and the latter were quickly changing from toes to talons, to say nothing of an incipient prolongation of the heel into a hind-claw.'* It is probably as well for us that the cradle is gone.

Finnie

to produce ponies with *'As much weight as possible, and as near the ground as it can be got.'* Nearby the beehive grain-drying kiln is restored.

Noss rises in a clean sweep culminating in vertical cliffs. Early tourists to Shetland were attracted to, and fascinated by, the cradle connecting Noss to the Holm of Noss, a large grass-covered stack. Said to date from the 17th century, by tradition a Foula man fixed the cradle to the Holm by scaling it from the sea, but chosing to return the way he came, he fell to his death. The cradle was removed in 1864. A National Nature Reserve notable for its bird life. *For access inquire in Lerwick: guidebook.*

Shetland Library

Top *The restored Pony Pund on Noss.* Right *The cradle of Noss drawn by John T Reid in 1867*

PAPA STOUR
'The big isle of the priests.' Low-lying flower-strewn meadow in the occupied area, moorland beyond. Notable coastline with stacks and caves.

Frau Stack, at the entrance to Housa Voe. '... *the Rubbish and Vestiges ... are yet to be seen'* of the tower where Thorvald Thoressen is said to have imprisoned his daughter to preserve her virtue *c.*1300. Variations of the tale conclude with a suitor scaling the stack and carrying the girl away. The name suggests, as elsewhere in Shetland, that it might have been a nunnery. At **Biggins**, excavations have revealed traces of a timber-lined and floored building, perhaps of the 10th century. Shetland's oldest document, dated 1299, mentions a dispute over ducal rents between Duke Hakon of Norway's bailiff Thorvald Thoressen and Ragnhild Simunsdatter of Papa Stour — the Duke's property. This altercation took place in the 'stofa' (principal room) of the Duke's house on the island. **Papa Stour Kirk**, 1806. '... *a neat structure* ...' harled with a tiny belfry, the inside is simple with a tiny loft. 17th-century gravestones. On the burn from Dutch Loch to Hamna Voe are the remains of two horizontal **water mills**.

Papa Stour Kirk

Ve Skerries Light, 1979, R J Mackay, Engineer. A reinforced concrete tower, above balcony level the lantern is re-used from the 1933 North Carr Lightship (now at the Scottish Fisheries Museum, Anstruther, Fife). This notorious reef claimed the trawler *Ben Doran* in 1930 with total loss of life.

Ve skerries light, under construction

On these treeless islands, there has been a long tradition of importing wood, so no doubt the stofa at Papa Stour would have used wood from Norway. Stock-Stove houses comprised a prefabricated, imported, timber roof and partition structure which was enclosed by locally built stone walls. The tradition continued until the 18th century.

TRONDRA AND BURRA

Hamnavoe, c. 1940

Shetland Museum

Trondra and the East and West Islands of Burra are long, narrow, islands which were connected to the Mainland by bridges in 1971. Trondra is first, the bridge allowing some expansion as a dormitory settlement after previous depopulation. On West Burra, **Hamnavoe** developed from six households in 1890 into what is arguably Shetland's only fishing village. Cottages in straight rows overlook the harbour. These rows, the Glen, Highmount, Roadside and others formed the backbone of the Hamnavoe layout. **Cottages**, mostly 1900-25, are generally low, two rooms and a central door with porch, felt roofs and plastered walls, often painted, over rubble or mass concrete. An amazing variety of porches include Gothic, classical and crenellated types and a great range of paint colours, traditionally surplus boat paints. Often extended with parallel blocks behind the main house. There is little subdivision of external space, vegetable plots shelter behind houses and a network of lanes wind through the village A unique environment in Shetland. **Sheltered Houses**, 1986, by Richard Gibson, a small group of cottages, two windows and porch, blending with the existing houses.

Hamnavoe Primary School, 1980, Richard Gibson
The classroom block steps back in shallow

Finnie

gabled, glazed, bays set off by a taller games
hall. Simple forms, white render, corrugated
roofs, much glass and strong colours. Curved
walls shelter outside play areas. In scale with
the village, casual and fragmented enough to fit.
RIBA Commendation in 1983. The **Church of
Scotland**, at Meal, 1907, is small and white
painted. It was built to serve the newly shifted
population.

*'At one point the two islands approach so near to
each other, as to be joined by a bridge composed
of loose timbers resting on two rude piles of
stones.'* Connected by causeway and bridge to
West and East Burra is the former **Bridge End
School**, a late 19th-century board school, which
occupies an islet in the sound.

Finnie

Top *Hamnavoe School.* Above
Hamnavoe Cottage. Left *Sheltered
houses, Hamnavoe*

Nearness to the **Burra Haaf**, a
large offshore fishing ground,
enabled Burra men to fish from
fourerns, four-men open boats,
rather than large sixerns. The
fourerns required less capital and
labour. They sailed off the sandy
beaches to the south of the isle but
by 1890 were being replaced by
deep-hulled smacks. Hamnavoe
provided the deep harbour. Huts and
barracks there gave way to
permanent houses when prosperity
allowed fishermen to give up their
crofts. Herring were fished from
smacks in the summer, haddock
from fourerns during winter. By the
1920s Burra was second in
importance to Lerwick as a fishing
centre. Still the base of the
fishermen, the fleet fishes largely
out of Scalloway.

Finnie

Papil
Kirkyard with the wreck of the **Kirk**, 1814. This
church replaced the third of Shetland's three
round-towered churches, perhaps 12th century,
St Laurence, demolished in the 1790s. Papil, as

Monks Stone from Papil in the Shetland Museum

the name indicates, was the site of an early religious community and from an 8th-century or earlier church here came the Monks and Papil stones. The former, which formed the side panel of a shrine, displays a procession of monks, (now in the Shetland Museum). The Papil Stone, a tall slab moved to the National Museum of Antiquities in Edinburgh, has a curious creature and more monks.

Right *Duncansclett.* Below *Windmill, South Havera*

Duncansclett at the road end has a good thatched cottage and out-buildings, surviving in a township amongst other roofless examples. Straw chimneys. Opposite, on East Burra can be seen the ruinous **Haa of Houss**, whose Laird, William Sinclair, fought against the Earl of Caithness at the battle of Summerdale in Orkney in 1529.

South Havera lies south of Burra. *'Hevera ... has the appearance of a high rock ... It accommodates five families, whose houses are frightfully situated on the brink of the precipice,'* and indeed they are, to avoid occupying the best of the land. Children, as well as animals, were tethered. Round openings above the porch doors supposedly allowed masts and spars to be stored in the roofspace. With no running water on the island, Shetland's only **Windmill** for grinding grain is situated on the summit. The wooden upperworks were turned to face the wind by being fitted into one of the openings around the hollow stone base. This mill is said to have been ineffective and grain was sent to the commercial mill at Kergord (Central Mainland). Finally abandoned in 1923, Havera, along with the islands of Papa, Oxna and Hildasay to the north, all now deserted, was dependent on fishing the Haaf. Hildasay did have a secondary industry in the granite quarry, extracting and exporting in the 19th century.

FOULA

The most rugged of these islands lies far to the west, with dark peaks against the sky. Steep hillsides sweep up from the east coast reaching 1373 ft at the Sneug. The land falls in vertical cliffs from as high as 1200 ft at the Kame, *the edge of the world*. Remote and difficult of access, Foula was the last of the islands to retain the Norn language, and still celebrates old Christmas and New Year in accordance with the Julian calendar. Isolation in the 20th century, and the lack of an adequate all-weather harbour for local fishermen, have resulted in the population dwindling to below 50. Mains electricity from an innovative wind and hydro scheme, an improved pier and a new school and community hall, all due for completion in 1990, hold hope for the future.

Foula's line of Norse udallers is said, improbably, to have died with 'Queen' Katherine Asmudder, born 1568, who lived in Denmark and visited the island annually. Forming part of the large Vaila estates of Mitchell of Girlsta and Scott of Melby from 1695, Foula was sold in 1895. Professor Ian B Stoughton Holbourn, classical scholar, historian and art lecturer became captivated with the island when passing *en route* to Iceland in 1899. He returned the following year and arranged the purchase. In subsequent years he spent his summers here.

'Dispecta est et Thule' — Thule too was seen, recorded Tacitus, historian to Agricola in the 1st century *AD*, when the Roman fleet first circumnavigated Britain and discovered the *Orcades*. From Orkney only the highest points of Shetland are visible, Fair Isle, Fitful Head and farthest but highest Foula.

Finnie

The Haa, Foula

The Haa, 18th century
Sitting over the island's only harbour (a tiny voe where the boats are hoisted out of the water), this plain house was built for the Scotts of Melby. Stuck on to the front is a grand Baronial porch begun by Holbourn, *c.*1910 but work stopped with only a turret corbel in place. **War Memorial**, *'the best in Shetland'*, is heavy

North Fair Isle Lighthouse

Finnie

Earl Rognvald
After Earl Magnus was murdered by
Earl Hakon on Egilsay c.1115, his
nephew Kali, called Rognvald, was
allocated Magnus's share by the
King in Norway. Rognvald sailed to
Shetland to claim his share of the
earldom but Hakon's son Paul
captured his fleet. Rognvald was
forced to return to Norway to
prepare a new fleet and then
returned to Shetland. Paul was
prepared and had set up beacons on
Fair Isle and North Ronaldsay.
Dagfinn on Fair Isle was tricked into
lighting his beacon by Rognvald's
father Kol sailing off Shetland in
small boats with large sails. For his
mistake the unfortunate Dagfinn
was axed by Thorstein of North
Ronaldsay. Next time Rognvald had
a follower infiltrate Fair Isle and
douse the becaon, and so Rognvald
landed unopposed in Orkney.

masonry with a pierced parapet. Erected by local
labour to Holbourn's design.

FAIR ISLE

Just as Martin Frobisher, in 1576, *en route* to
the North-West passage gained *'a sight of Fair
Yle'* so do present-day travellers: a glimpse
through clouds or silhouetted against the
evening sky from the *North Boat*. The island is
distinctly divided between northern scattald and
southern croftland by an ancient 'feelie' dyke
and, alongside, its drystone replacement. The
island's ferry is hauled from storm waters at
North Haven, overlooked by the **Bird
Observatory**, 1970, which replaced George
Waterston's 1948 set-up housed in the ex-naval
huts on the beach. Passionately interested in
birds, Waterston bought the island after the
Second World War, since being on a migration
crossroads, the island can be host to rare
species. The George Waterston Memorial Centre
forms the island's museum within *the Auld
Schule*. The island is now a property of the
National Trust for Scotland. Britain's first
commerical **Aerogenerator** supplements the
island's diesel-powered electricity supply.
Decorative portholes, from the unfortunate
Black Watch, can be seen on an outbuilding at
Stoneybreck.

North Fair Isle Light, 1891,
David & Charles Stevenson
A clifftop light of dumpy tower on a flat-roofed
base. The keepers' houses were demolished after
automation c.1980. A sundial, to check lighting
times, remains.

Church services alternate between the **Kirk**,
1892, plain and white harled, and the
Methodist Chapel, 1886, in rubble. The latter's
plain interior is livened by bright stained glass
of 1936.

South Fair Isle Light, 1891,
David & Charles Stevenson
All neat and white within its enclosing wall.
Similar to the north light but being near sea
level the tower is higher. The keepers' houses
are extant. A 19th-century semaphore, used to
signal to passing warships, stands on the hill
behind.

The Haa, 18th century
Homely, low and lime-washed with deepset
windows, massive chimneys and crowsteps. The

roof timbers have been salvaged from wrecks. Walter Scott was entertained here, in 1814, by the Master of Fair Isle.

The 96 merks of land which formed **Fair Isle** were acquired sometime in the early 17th century by the Sinclairs of Quendale. When the Quendale estates was bankrupted in 1766 the Stewarts of Brough in Orkney bought the island. It reverted back to Shetland ownership in 1866 under the Bruces of Sumburgh. Under the National Trust for Scotland the population has now stabilised (after a former threat of evacuation) and the island is tidy.

Fair Isle knitwear is probably of Norse origin but folklore connects the patterns to the shipwrecked Spaniards of *El Gran Grifon*, the flagship of the transport squadron of the Spanish Armada which was wrecked at Stroms Hellier. 300 sailors became billeted on the 100 or so islanders for six weeks before they could be taken off in September 1588. *'We found the island peopled by seventeen households in huts, more like hovels than anything else ...'*

Finnie

Left *Fair Isle Haa, sheep rock behind.* Below *South Light, Fair Isle and semaphore*

Finnie

ACKNOWLEDGEMENTS

The author would like to thank the many people who assisted in this volume. Particular thanks are due to Brian Smith, Shetland Archivist, for his diligent research and manuscript reading; Tommy Watt of the Shetland Museum who searched out photographs from the museum's vast collection; Charles McKean for his enthusiasm, his commitment to this volume and the series and particularly for his patience in the face of my ongoing delays; Duncan McAra; Margaret Wilson and Dorothy Smith for administration. Hilary Harmer gave freely the information she obtained, in Shetland, on a similar quest to that of the author.

The City of Aberdeen Art Gallery; Mr G D Atkinson; Dennis Coutts; the Highlands & Islands Development Board; Historic Buildings and Monuments; SDD; George Hunter; John Rylands University Library of Manchester; National Library of Scotland; Northern Lighthouse Board; Old Haa at Burravoe; Michael Peterson; Property Services Agency; Royal Commission on the Ancient and Historical Monuments of Scotland; Laura Stewart Sandison; John Scott; Shetland Library; Shetland Museum; and Ena Tait all kindly gave me permission to publish some of their treasures. Sources of illustration are noted against each.

Great assistance in the compilation of the volume was given by the following: Henry Anderton; Mrs J Baisley; Mrs V Bruce; Rhoda Bulter; Lt-Col R N R Cross; Gordon Dargie; Professor Gordon Donaldson; Faulkner Browns; Gillian Finnie; Iain Finnie; Professor Derek Flinn; Barbara Garriock; Richard Gibson; Ian Gow; Alastair Hamilton; June and James Henry; Peter Hick; John C Hope; Mr J Jamieson; G R M Kennedy & Partners; Mrs C Leslie; Loganair pilots; John Lucock; Norrie Mills; the late Richard Moira; Leslie D Morrison & Partners; Wendy and John Scott; Isobel Sparrow; Jim Sutherland; Stella Sutherland; Dr David Walker; and many other people who generously gave their time, advice and hospitality.

References

The arrangement of this guide precludes the normal methods of reference. The following list includes the principal sources which have been used in this publication.

BALNEAVES, Elizabeth, **The Windswept Isles**; BUTLER, David, **The Island of Noss**; BYRON, Reginald, **Sea Change;** CAMERON, A D, **Go Listen to the Crofters**; CANT R, G, **The Medieval Churches and Chapels of Shetland**; COWIE, Robert, **Shetland**; CRAWFORD, Barbara E, **Essays in Shetland History**; CRAWFORD, J M, **Parish of Lerwick**; DONALDSON, Gordon, **Shetland life under Earl Patrick**; EDMONSTON, Arthur, **A View of the Ancient and Present State of the Zetland Islands**; FENTON, Alexander, **The Northern Isles: Orkney and Shetland;** FLINN, Derek, **Travellers in a bygone Shetland**; GIFFORD, Thomas, **Historical Description of the Zetland Islands in the year 1733;** GRANT, F J, **Zetland Family Histories;** HAY, Geoffrey, **Post-Reformation Churches;** HIBBERT, Samuel, **A Description of the Shetland Islands**; HOLBOURN, I B C, **The Isle of Foula;** HOWARTH, D M, **The Shetland Bus;** IRVINE, James W, **The Dunrossness Story, Lerwick, Up Helly Aa;** JOHNSON, Robert, **A Shetland Country Merchant;** LEIRFALL, J, **West over Sea;** LINKLATER, Eric, **Orkney and Shetland;** LOW, George, **A Tour Through the Islands of Orkney and Schetland;** MAIR, Craig, **A Star for Seamen;** MANSON, T, **Humours of a Peat Commission;** MANSON, T, **Lerwick during the last half century**; MARTIN, Simon, **The other Titanic;** MUIR, T S, **Shetland Revisited: an ecclesiological sketch;** MUNRO, R W, **Scottish Lighthouses;** NELSON, G M, **History of Tingwall Kirk;** NICOLSON, James R, **Shetland; Orkneyinga Saga;** PLOYEN, Christian, **Reminiscences of a Voyage to Shetland, Orkney and Scotland;** POINTS, G A, **A Concise Guide to Historic Shetland;** REID, J T, **Art Rambles in Shetland**; RITCHIE, Anna, **Exploring Scotland's Heritage: Orkney and Shetland;** ROUSSELL, Aage, **Norse Building Customs;** SANDISON, W, **A Shetland Merchant's day book in 1762;** SAVAGE, Peter, **Lorimer and the Edinburgh Craft Designers;** SCOTT, Sir Walter, **The Pirate, Northern Light; Shetland Folk Book;** SIBBALD, Sir R, **A Description of the Isles of Orknay and Zetland;** SMITH, Brian, **Shetland Archaeology; Old Statistical Account; New Statistical Account; Third Statistical Account;** TUDOR, John R, **The Orkneys and Shetland: their past and present state;** WILSON, J, **A Voyage round Scotland**.